VAN BUREN DISTRICT LIBRARY
DECAT

P9-CDK-259

DISCARDED

Contemporary Discourse
in the Field of
ASTRONOMY ™

The Size, Composition, and Surface Features of the Planets Orbiting the Sun

An Anthology of Current Thought

Edited by Ellen Foxxe

The Rosen Publishing Group, Inc., New York

523.2
Siz

Published in 2006 by The Rosen Publishing Group, Inc.
29 East 21st Street, New York, NY 10010

Copyright © 2006 by The Rosen Publishing Group, Inc.

First Edition

All rights reserved. No part of this book may be reproduced
in any form without permission in writing from the publisher,
except by a reviewer.

Library of Congress Cataloging-in-Publication Data

The size, composition, and surface features of the planets
orbiting the sun: an anthology of current thought/edited by
Ellen Foxxe.
    p. cm.—(Contemporary discourse in the field of astronomy)
ISBN 1-4042-0394-X (lib. bdg.)
1. Solar system. 2. Planetology. 3. Earth—Origin.
I. Foxxe, Ellen. II. Series.
QB501.S55 2006
523.2—dc22

                                                    2004026663

Manufactured in the United States of America

On the cover: Bottom right: the Sun shining behind Earth and
the Moon. Bottom left: Galileo Galilei. Center left: the Dumbell
Nebula. Top right: solar flares.

CONTENTS

Introduction

As long as there have been people on Earth, they have looked at the sky and observed the motions of the planets, wondering about the significance of the planets that traversed the sky. Many earlier civilizations endowed the distant planets with mystical or religious significance, and a number of ancient civilizations carefully tracked the motion of the planets and created systems based on their movement to mark the passing of time. For instance, the ancient Maya tracked not only the movement of the Sun and Moon but also that of Venus and Jupiter. And it was in 2136 BC in ancient China that the first eclipse of the Sun was recorded.

Since ancient times, people have sought to expand their knowledge of the planets. The ancient Greeks named the planets and plotted their courses across the sky. Five planets—Mercury, Venus, Mars, Jupiter, and Saturn—can be observed with the naked eye. Modern astronomy began in 1543, when Nicolaus Copernicus developed a model of the solar system with a stationary Sun at its center, orbited by the observable planets. In 1609 and 1619, Johannes Kepler published works describing the three laws of planetary motion. From 1609 to 1610, Galileo became the first person to use a telescope to observe the planets. He discovered that planets were spheres, and he identified moons around Jupiter. His work provided important evidence to support Copernicus's claim that the solar system consisted of the Sun with the planets orbiting around it. This concept was met with much controversy at a time when religious authorities considered Earth to be the center of the universe.

Eventually, the scientific evidence won out and the model of the solar system with six planets orbiting the Sun was accepted. The English astronomer Sir William Herschel is credited with discovering Uranus in 1781. Neptune was discovered in 1846 by astronomers at the Berlin Observatory working at the behest of French mathematician Urbain-Jean-Joseph Le Verrier. In the ensuing years, astronomers, relying on ever-improving telescopes, discovered new planetary characteristics, including Jupiter's famous Great Red Spot, polar ice caps on Mars, and the rings around Saturn. The ninth planet, Pluto, was discovered by astronomers at the Lowell Observatory in Arizona in February 1930.

Radio-wave observations began to be used in the 1950s to expand our knowledge of planets. People and robotic probes started going into space in the 1960s, sending back images and data that shed new light on the surfaces and compositions of the planets. The first such space probe was *Mariner 4*, which sent back data on Mars in 1965. The first probes to leave the solar system were the twin spacecraft *Pioneer 10* and *Pioneer 11*, launched in 1972 and 1973, respectively. The Hubble Space Telescope, launched in 1990, has provided images from the solar system and galaxies beyond. In the next few years, probes such as those of the Jet Propulsion Laboratory's New Horizons project (aimed at exploring Pluto and the Kuiper Belt), will provide new information on the bodies at the edge of our solar system, sending back images and data that will no doubt change yet again what we think we know about the planets.

As we have extended our scientific reach from observing our nearby neighboring planets to sending probes to the edges of our solar system and beyond, we have learned vast amounts of information about the nature of the planets. Our explorations have produced many surprises; they have also raised many new questions that have yet to be answered. The articles in this book provide insight into some of the newest discoveries in the field of astronomy and explore these new questions.

Among some of these puzzles are, is there really water on Mars, and if so, what does that signify? Is Pluto really a planet? Why are Neptune and Uranus orbiting so far out at the edge of the solar system, given their composition? What do the surfaces of Venus, Jupiter, and the planets at the far reaches of the solar system look like? Which planets have rings, what are these rings composed of, and how did they form? Are there more planets lurking in the Kuiper Belt at the boundary of the solar system? These and other cutting-edge questions are examined in the following articles.

This book is divided into five chapters. The first, "Earth and the Neighbors Next Door," examines such questions as what modern technology can tell us about the surface, composition, and size of Earth and its nearest neighbors, Mercury and Venus. It covers such scientific questions as how Earth's surface was formed and why there are so few impact craters on Earth, whether there are volcanoes on Mercury, and what the surface of Venus is like and why. The second chapter, "The Red Planet," considers questions relating to Mars, such as whether there is water on Mars's surface and what form it takes. The third chapter, "Ring Around the Planets," explores issues surrounding the discovery that Saturn is not alone in having rings. It covers which planets have rings and recent theories proposed to explain what these rings are made of and how they formed. It also takes a look at some of the most recent information on the nature of the surface and composition of the ringed planets. The fourth chapter, "Giants in the Sky," takes a look at the gas giant planets—Saturn, Jupiter, Uranus, and Neptune—and explores what new data has to tell us about their origin, composition, and sometimes puzzling orbits. The final chapter, "At the Edge of the Solar System," explores such issues as whether or not Pluto is really a planet, the nature of the Kuiper Belt, and the ring of matter at the edge of our solar system that served as the nursery for the planets in our solar system. It covers the discovery of planetlike objects at the edge of our solar system and beyond, and what they have to tell us about the nature of the known planets nearer home.

The articles in this book provide an exciting, captivating, and surprising look at the planets around us.—*EF*

1 Earth and the Neighbors Next Door

When we look at the night sky through binoculars, the various planets orbiting our Sun all appear to be different colors. For instance, Mars looks red. In earlier times, people observed these variations in color and believed they had symbolic significance. In the eighteenth century, astronomers first understood that planets appear to be colored because they reflect sunlight. But why do they appear to be different colors? The colors we see when looking at the planets provide us with valuable information about what's on the surface of the various planets. For instance, when seen from space, Earth appears to be blue because of its atmosphere (not because of the water on its surface), while Mars gets it orange color from the iron oxide in its soil. The following article examines the various planets in our solar system and reveals what we can tell about them from the colors we observe as they traverse the night sky.—EF

"Sky Lights: Colors Reveal What's Brewing on Other Planets"
by Bob Berman
Discover, December 2001

As December begins, simply pointing binoculars at bright, ocher Mars places dim, lime-tinged Uranus in the same field of view. That red-and-green traffic light conjunction, low in the southwest after sunset, provides an easy way for novices to find the rarely seen Uranus. The conjunction also highlights the two most deeply tinted planets, raising an age-old question: What gives planets their distinctive colors? Throughout most of history, celestial tints were no more than Rorschach tests of human cultures. Ancients looked at the somewhat reddish hue of Mars and saw fire or blood, leaving us with warlike Mars associations that are still evident in terms such as martial arts and court martial. By the 18th century, scientists recognized that planets shine because they reflect sunlight. As Isaac Newton had demonstrated, sunlight contains all the colors of the rainbow, which when blended together appear white to the human eye. A surface retains this neutral whiteness if all colors bounce back equally. Conversely, any distinct coloration shows that some portion of the rainbow has been absorbed, and that provides intriguing information about what exists on the planet's surface.

For example, Earth looks blue not because of its oceans but because of the atmosphere. Astronauts looking down at our planet see the same azure we do when gazing up at the sky. The cause is atmospheric molecules that are just the right size to scatter the sun's short, blue wavelengths. Air scatters blue light 10 times more readily than it scatters red.

Martian air, by contrast, is too thin to scatter much light. This is evident from telescopic images of the planet, although hints of blue peek out around the edges of the disk, where we can peer through the thickest slice of its atmosphere. The dominant hue of Mars, yellow-orange, comes from the iron oxide—ordinary rust—in the soil, which gets kicked up by 100-mile-per-hour winds that episodically change the sky from blue to a bizarre pink. Every decade or two, global storms blow the rusty dust around the entire planet; one such storm started last July and may still be raging. These dust bowls give Mars a more golden tint.

Distant, frigid Uranus derives its vivid coloration from methane, the same gas that sometimes hovers in an invisible cloud over marshes on Earth. The compound is composed of one carbon atom bound to four hydrogen atoms. Methane absorbs red light, so copious quantities of the gas in Uranus' atmosphere boost its blue-scattering effect, painting the world a dramatic aqua. When viewed through binoculars, the planet's color appears further amplified because at low light levels our retinas respond to blue-green far more readily than they do to any other color.

Pan to pale Jupiter—an easy task, as it reaches its closest approach of the year on December 31, when it rises in the east at sunset and rides high and dazzling at midnight. Even small telescopes reveal its famous Great

Red Spot, more like a weak pink spot, and the faint bands crossing the off-white disk. On a gas-planet such as Jupiter, these are the colors of turmoil. Warm colors denote upheaval and chemical activity. Observations from NASA's Galileo space probe suggest Jupiter's atmosphere is driven by fast-rising, rapidly cooling gases and by charged particles raining down from the planet's powerful magnetic field. Scientists still haven't identified the exact chemistry behind the colors, but it likely includes compounds of sulfur and phosphorus, the stuff of kitchen matches.

To the right of Jupiter, Saturn shines brighter than at any time in the past quarter century, yet it displays almost no color. That blandness betrays another set of conditions: lots of stability, little methane. So if Santa doesn't bring you a chemistry set, no matter. This month the sky provides its own.

Reprinted with permission from *Discover* magazine.

When Mariner 10 explored the surface of Mercury in 1974, it left unresolved the question of whether the widespread plains on the planet's surface formed as a result of volcanic activity or were basins that were formed as the result of impact from meteorites. The authors of the following article recalibrated the Mariner 10 color image data in order to identify distinct color units on Mercury's surface. They

*analyzed this data to see what minerals were
present and found that the iron content and
soil maturity indicated the presence of volcanic deposits on Mercury's surface. In
addition, they found that materials associated
with some impact craters were similar in composition to material found in the lunar crust.
Their findings suggest that Mercury has
undergone a development process similar to
that of the other terrestrial planets (those with
rocky surfaces), such as Earth and Mars, and
Earth's moon.—EF*

"Recalibrated Mariner 10 Color Mosaics: Implications for Mercurian Volcanism"
by Mark S. Robinson and Paul G. Lucey
Science, January 10, 1997

Recalibration of Mariner 10 color image data allows
the identification of distinct color units on the mercurian surface. We analyze these data in terms of opaque
mineral abundance, iron content, and soil maturity
and find color units consistent with the presence of
volcanic deposits on Mercury's surface. Additionally,
materials associated with some impact craters have
been excavated from a layer interpreted to be deficient in opaque minerals within the crust, possibly
analogous to the lunar anorthosite crust. These observations suggest that Mercury has undergone complex
differentiation like the other terrestrial planets and
the Earth's moon.

One unresolved question from the Mariner 10 exploration of Mercury is whether widespread plains deposits formed due to volcanism or basin formation-related impact ejecta.[1-3] We recalibrated and analyzed the Mariner 10 first encounter approach color data to address this fundamental issue. Previous analyses of Mariner 10 images defined color units on Mercury which indicated that color boundaries often did not correspond to photogeologic units, and no low albedo relatively blue mercurian materials were found that correspond to lunar mare deposits.[4, 5] The calibration employed in these earlier studies did not completely remove vidicon blemishes and radiometric residuals. These artifacts were sufficiently severe that the authors presented an interpretive color unit map overlaid on monochromatic mosaics while publishing only a subset of the color ratio coverage of Mercury.[4-7] We derived a refined calibration that increased the signal-to-noise ratio of these mercurian image data. These recalibrated image mosaics show the complete ultraviolet (UV) orange color data for this portion of Mercury. We interpret these recalibrated data in terms of the current paradigm of visible color reflectance for iron-bearing silicate regoliths.[5, 6, 8]

The Mariner 10 vidicon imaging system was spatially nonuniform in bias and dark current, as well as being nonlinear at the extremes of the light transfer curve.[9] Prelaunch flat field images acquired at varying exposure times allowed for the derivation of a nonlinearity and sensitivity nonuniformity correction, while an average of inflight images of deep space corrected for system offset.[10] We utilized low-contrast Mariner 10 images of the venusian atmosphere to identify vidicon blemishes and create a stencil from which affected areas were simply deleted from all the mercurian images. Two spatially redundant mercurian mosaic sequences were processed for each filter and thus little areal coverage was lost due to the blemish deletion procedure. Instead of overlaying each image during the mosaicking, the images were averaged so that each pixel was formed from one to seven frames. The data were resampled to 3 km per pixel (original data were 2 to 3 km per pixel) centered at the subspacecraft point to enhance the signal-to-noise ratio of the mosaics. The averaging technique, conservative resampling, and blemish deletion reduced the effects of system noise, bit errors, and calibration residuals such that subtle color units can be identified. Absolute calibration was derived by photometrically normalizing the images to 0 [degrees] phase, using the equations of Hapke,[11] and deriving a coefficient such that the disc-integrated average of the orange mosaic (575 nm) matches the Earth-based telescopic, disc-integrated 554-nm geometric albedo of 0.14.[12] The disc-integrated value from the photometrically normalized UV (355 nm) mosaic was adjusted to match a value 0.6 that of the orange value, which corresponds to the mercurian spectral slope derived from Earth-based measurements.[13]

Terrestrial-based remote sensing studies[14–16] and photogeology[3] indicate that Mercury has a silicate crust bearing minerals such as feldspars, pyroxenes, and olivine.[4–6] Rava and Hapke[5] provided an interpretive framework to understand the spectral properties of Mercury, based on the assumption of a lunar-like surface composition. In general, the addition of ferrous iron to a silicate mineral or glass darkens the material and reddens the visible spectral slope (decreases the UV/orange color ratio[17, 18] [see Fig. 1 in original article]). This correlation of albedo and color ratio due to variations in ferrous iron is mimicked by variation of maturity of lunar, and likely mercurian, soils. In the course of the space-weathering maturation process, vacuum reduction of ferrous iron to submicroscopic native iron causes relatively blue immature soils to darken and spectrally redden.[19] Thus, since the Mariner 10 data examined here consist of only two wavelengths, it is problematic to decouple the spectral effects of ferrous iron content and maturity due to space weathering. However, increases in the abundance of spectrally neutral opaque minerals, such as ilmenite, tend to darken but decrease the spectral redness of silicate soils[5, 20] [see Fig. 1 in original article]. Rotation of two key parameters (UV/orange ratio versus orange albedo), so that the two trends are perpendicular to the axes, should result in decoupling the effects of ferrous iron plus maturity and opaque mineral abundance variations. This coordinate rotation results in images of two parameters [see Fig. 2 in original article], one sensitive to ferrous iron plus maturity and the other to opaque mineral content.[18] It is apparent that spatially coherent structures in the parameter 1 image (iron plus maturity, [see Fig. 2C in original article]) are mostly associated with crater rays and ejecta, suggesting that this parameter is dominated by maturity variations. The spatial patterns in the parameter 2 image (opaque content, [see Fig. 2D in original article]) are not related to ejecta or crater rays and so are most likely compositional units formed by other geologic processes.

Widespread plains deposits have been identified on Mercury and it is controversial whether these deposits are related to large impact basin formation or volcanism.[1-3] Impact-related origins have been proposed for the mercurian plains because they do not show high-contrast albedo boundaries with the surroundings, analogous to impact-related light plains on the moon, such as the Cayley formation, which appear to be largely remobilized local material.[2, 3] However, volcanic plains deposits do occur on the moon, such as the Apennine Bench formation[21, 22] with distinct composition and do not exhibit high-contrast albedo boundaries; thus, albedo is not a definitive diagnostic indicator of composition or compositional differences. Nevertheless, compositional contrast (detectable by color differences) with surrounding material remains a key indicator of volcanic versus basin-related origin for a plains deposit.

Our recalibration has reduced the systematic noise in the Mariner 10 data set such that correlations between morphologic and color boundaries can be discerned. A plains unit west of Rudaki crater is defined by embayment relations of distinct color boundaries [See Fig. 3 in original article] that correspond to previously mapped plains boundaries.[23] The Rudaki plains have an intermediate opaque index and overlies darker materials that have higher opaque indices. These spectral relationships suggest that the Rudaki-type plains are compositionally distinct from their surroundings and demonstrate that at least some of the extensive plains units on Mercury were emplaced as volcanic flows [See Fig. 3 in original article].

The Rudaki plains (and similar plains [seen in Fig. 2 in original article]) do not appear as anomalies in the ferrous iron plus maturity image [See Fig. 2C in original article], indicating that they have similar FeO contents to the rest of the mercurian crust in this image. The mercurian global crustal abundance of FeO has been estimated to be less than 6% by weight.[13-15] Sprague et al.[15] tentatively identified a basalt-like material in this hemisphere with Earth-based thermal infrared measurements, while later microwave measurements indicated a paucity of really significant basaltic materials on Mercury.[16] From the Mariner 10 data presented here, we cannot make a definitive identification of a low iron basaltic material; however, the spectral parameters, stratigraphic relations, and morphology are consistent with such a material.

Volcanic materials can be ballistically emplaced as pyroclastic deposits. Figure 3A [see original article] shows dark blue material exhibiting diffuse boundaries consistent with ballistically emplaced material. There is no impact crater central to these deposits and they straddle a linear segment of a ring of Homer basin that could serve as a weakness in the crust, allowing magma to reach the surface, morphology consistent with a pyroclastic origin as explosive fissure eruptions. A similar spectral unit occurs northwest of the crater Lermontov [see Fig. 3B in original article]; both exhibit relatively blue color, high opaque index, and low albedo, which is consistent with a more mafic material. If these units are pyroclastic in origin, they represent not only a distinct composition, but an important clue to the volatile history of the planet.

One of the most striking features shown in Figs. 2 and 3 [see original article] is the Kuiper-Muraski crater complex. Kuiper, superposed on the crater Muraski [see Fig. 3B in original article], is one of the youngest large impact craters on Mercury.[3] Kuiper has an opaque index equivalent to Muraski, but the iron-maturity parameter indicates that Kuiper is relatively immature, consistent with its fresher morphology, thus explaining the color difference (relatively blue). The opaque index for both materials is very low, possibly similar to a lunar soil formed from an anorthositic crust. For the portions of Mercury shown in Fig. 2 [see original article], the regions with the lowest opaque index are associated with craters, consistent with excavation of a layer at depth that is deficient in opaque minerals [see Fig. 2D in original article] resurfaced by later processes. This layer may be analogous to an ancient lunar anorthosite crust. Consistent with this hypothesis, Earth-based remote sensing has tentatively identified anorthosite on Mercury.[15]

The distinct color units identified here suggest that the mercurian crust is compositionally heterogeneous and poorly mixed on the scale of the Mariner 10 data (3 km).

Additionally, the suggestion of really significant volcanic materials on Mercury implies that volcanism may have played a significant role in global cooling and thus, thermal models of the planet might be reexamined.[16, 24]

References and Notes

1. B. C. Murray, J. Geophys. Res. 80, 2342 (1975); B. C. Murray et al., Science 185, 169 (1974); R. G. Strom, Phys. Earth Planet Inter. 15, 156 (1977); D. Dzurisin J. Geophys. Res. 83, 4883 (1978); W. S. Keiffer and B. C. Murray, Icarus 72, 477 (1987).

2. D. E. Wilhelms, Icarus 28, 551 (1976).

3. P. D. Spudis and J. E. Guest, in Mercury, F. Vilas, C. R. Chapman, M. S. Matthews, Eds. (Univ. of Arizona Press, Tucson, AZ, 1988), pp. 118-164.

4. B. Hapke, C. Christman, B. Rava, J. Mosher, Proc. Lunar Planet. Sci. Conf. 11, 817 (1980).

5. B. Rava and B. Hapke, Icarus 71, 397 (1987).

6. B. Hapke, G. E. Danielson, K. Klaasen, L. Wilson, J. Geophys. Res. 80, 2431 (1975).

7. B. Hapke, J. Atmos. Sci. 33,1803 (1976).

8. M. J. Cintala, J. Geophys. Res. 97, 947 (1992).

9. M. Benesh and M. Morrill, Jet Propul. Lab. Doc. 615-148 (1973); G. E. Danielson, K. P. Klaasen, J. L. Anderson, J. Geophys. Res. 80, 2357 (1975); J. M. Soha et al., ibid., p. 2394.

10. M. S. Robinson, B. R. Hawke, P. G. Lucey, J. Geophys. Res. 97, 18265 (1992). The offset (signal inherent in the imaging system when no photons are impinging on the detector) was derived by averaging images acquired during the color sequence where Mercury did not appear in the frame—the camera was imaging nothing but deep space. As a test of the stability of the offset during the imaging sequence, the average offset image was subtracted from each frame of space acquired during the color sequence and no significant drift was measurable (camera A average residual was 0.3 DN; camera B average residual was 0.1 DN; possible range of DN 0-255). Examination of overlap between calibrated frames (dark corrected and linearized) revealed a maximum mismatch of 5 %, with the average being 2 %. Averaging areas of overlap between multiple frames reduced this residual in the final mosaics.

11. Applying Hapke modeling [B. W. Hapke, Icarus 67, 264 (1986)] with parameters derived for the moon [P. Helfenstein and J. Veverka, ibid. 72, 343 (1987); (12)] and those derived for Mercury resulted in overcorrection at the mercurian poles.

Previous work with Galileo solid-state imager data has shown that [theta] (theta bar) can be adjusted to compensate for such an overcorrection [A. S. McEwen and T. L. Becker, Lunar Planet. Sci. XXIV, 955 (1993)] Iterative adjustment and visual inspection of the photometric flatness of the mercurian mosaic led us to use the following values for the Hapke parameters: w = 0.21, h = 0.07, [B.sub.0] = 2.0, b = 0.29, c = 0.39, and [theta] (theta bar) = 15. It is known that the lunar photometric function varies subtly as a function of wavelength and composition (see McEwen and Becker, above), and the same is most likely true for Mercury. However such minor effects will not hinder our identification of relative local color boundaries, which are key to the science presented here.

12. B. Hapke, Phys. Earth Planet. Inter. 15, 264 (1977); J. Veverka, P. Helfenstein, B. Hapke, J. D. Goguen, in Mercury, F. Vilas, C. Chapman, M. S. Mathews, Eds. (Univ. of Arizona Press, Tucson, 1988) pp. 37-58.

13. F. Vilas, in Mercury, F. Vilas, C. Chapman, M. S. Mathews Eds. (Univ. of Arizona Press, Tucson, 1988) pp. 59-76.

14. T. B. McCord and J. B. Adams, Icarus 17, 585 (1972); F. Vilas and T. B. McCord, ibid. 28, 593 (1976); F. Vilas, M. A. Leake, W. W. Mendell, ibid. 59, 60 (1984); F. Vilas, ibid. 64, 133 (1985).

15. A. L. Sprague, R. W. H. Kozlowski, F. C. Witteborn, D. P. Cruikshank, D. H. Wooden, ibid. 109, 156 (1994).

16. R. Jeanloz, D. L. Mitchell, A. L. Sprague, I. de Pater, Science 268, 1455 (1995).

17. J. B. Adams, J. Geophys. Res. 79, 4829 (1974).

18. P. G. Lucey, D. T. Blewett, J. L. Johnson, G. J. Taylor, B. R. Hawke, Lunar Planet. Sci. XXVII, 781 (1996).

19. B. Hapke, W. Cassidy, E. Wells, Moon 13, 339 (1975); B. Hapke, in (12); R. V. Morris, Proc. Lunar Planet. Sci. Conf. 11, 1697 (1980).

20. M. P. Charette, T. B. McCord, C. Pieters, J. B. Adams, J. Geophys. Res. 79, 1605 (1974); E. Wells and B. Hapke, Science 195, 977 (1977).

21. P. D. Spudis, Proc. Lunar Planet. Sci. Conf. 9, 3379 (1978).

22. B. R. Hawke and J. W. Head, ibid., p. 3285.

23. R. A. DeHon, D. H. Scott, J. R. Underwood, U.S. Geol. Surv. Misc. Invest. Series Map I-1233 (1981).

24. T. Spohn, Icarus 90, 222 (1991).

25. We find that the highest albedo materials in the mosaic (that is, crater Kuiper) are only about two times the global average (0.29 versus 0.14, respectively), whereas Hapke et al. (6) report the floor of Kuiper to be about three times the global average (0.45 versus 0.14). We are unable to explain the discrepancy satisfactorily and assume that it is due to improvements in our calibration.

Earth and the Neighbors Next Door

"Land Before Time"
by Peter Weiss
Earth, February 1998

*Scientists are not in agreement on how the continental
crust, or Earth's land masses, were formed. Some feel it
developed gradually, though others believe the Earth had
its own "big bang" and formed the crust in a sudden burst
as early as four billion years ago.*

The first snapshots of our planet's face are rocks
roughly four billion years old. They go back a long way.
But Earth was actually born well before then, so there
are a lot of precious early moments—about a half billion years' worth—missing from the family album. It's
as if no one got out the camera until the tyke was
already a toddler.

What was our newborn planet's face like? Did she
have a prominent forehead? A pointy nose? Or was the
distinctive surface of the planet—the continental
crust—still waiting to appear?

Continental crust is the geologist's term for Earth's
land masses. It's made of granitelike rock and stands
tall, averaging twenty-eight miles in thickness. (The
crust under the oceans, by comparison, averages only
five miles thick.) So this is not an insignificant part of
the planet. Surprisingly, scientists can't agree on how
and when it got here.

For some, such as Scott McLennan of the State
University of New York in Stony Brook, the answer

seems fairly straightforward. Since there are precious few rocks approaching four billion years in age, there couldn't have been crust before then. Indeed, the ages of most existing continental rocks indicate that things didn't really start growing until about three billion years ago, he contends, and have proceeded in fits and starts ever since. "It comes down to Occam's razor," says McLennan. "If you have no evidence of ancient continental crust and don't need to explain the data, why propose it?"

Unless, of course, you've actually discovered the world's oldest rocks and think there's more where they came from. Just last year Samuel Bowring of the Massachusetts Institute of Technology and Ian Williams of the Australia National University in Canberra found rocks in northern Canada that are at least four billion years old. But it's what Bowring and his colleagues haven't found that points them toward truly ancient crust: missing elements. When rocks form from the underlying layer, the mantle, they take certain elements with them when they go. And rocks representing the mantle of very early Earth happen to be poor in these exact elements.

Something left the mantle, Bowring says, and that something became the land beneath your feet. This crust all formed in a burst of creation starting as early as four billion years ago—in Earth's very own "Big Bang"—and ever since then it has been churned around and reshaped on the outside of the planet.

The debate itself has been churning for a while, and it hasn't always been pleasant. Richard

Armstrong, a geologist then at Yale, proposed in the late 1960s that the crust appeared in an early burst. His proposal was panned by the gradual growth proponents, but he held on to it tenaciously until his death of cancer in 1991. Before dying, he lashed out at his critics in a polemic in an Australian earth science journal that charged them with perpetuating myths. He died "a bitter man," says Bowring.

The trace elements have given the proposal new life. And they've given opponents a new target. Some have questioned the accuracy of these experiments. At a meeting of crust researchers last year, scientists leapt to their feet and demanded that Victoria Bennett, one of the early-burst advocates, admit she was wrong and retract her results. "I certainly did not expect the vigor of the attack," Bennett recalls. She also refused to back down.

A Matter of Timing

The two groups do agree on some points. One of them is the basic way that crust is created. Making continental granites, when you start from mantle rocks, requires at least two stages of melting and crystallization when less dense ingredients can separate out and rise. The motions of crustal plates, or plate tectonics, give ample opportunity for these stages to happen.

At long volcanic ridges on the ocean bottoms, magma wells up and solidifies to form new ocean bottom—the basaltic oceanic crust, which is much denser than the stuff of continents—that pushes away from the ridges. At deep-ocean trenches thousands of miles away, cooled slabs of that crust nose back into the mantle, or subduct. Their descent causes the mantle above them to melt. That's stage one: The melted materials push upward and form precursors to the stuff of new continents. Then comes stage two. At these shallow levels, additional heat from the mantle triggers a new round of melting, and when the rock cools it forms into granite.

Fresh crust also forms in the mid-oceans over hotspots, such as the one beneath Hawaii. At those hotspots, a fixed well of magma punches through the ocean crust, piling up new volcanic islands or submarine mountains and plateaus. These features ride the ocean-crust conveyor belt to the trenches where they are too buoyant to be tugged back into the interior. The trench edges plane them off and they pile up as new land at the continents' margins.

There's another point of agreement. Although no one knows for certain when plate tectonics began, both sides concur that there was a time on early Earth, at least briefly, when there were neither plate tectonics nor continental crust.

More than 4.5 billion years ago, the embryonic, hot planet could sustain only some sort of primitive, short-lived crust. The planet had to be very hot back then, which would mean any crust was very thin and weak, because it had just formed from high-energy crashes of debris zipping through space. Today the ancient, crater-scarred surfaces of rocky, sister planets Mercury, Venus, and Mars attest to the hellish bombardment that was going on until roughly 3.8 billion years ago.

With that incoming, high-energy barrage, it would have been hard to develop a thicker, continent-laden crust. All Venus was able to sustain, for example, was a thin basaltic crust very much like the brittle layers beneath Earth's oceans. For the same reasons, because of the heat and constant impacts, Earth's earliest crust would have been a shallow, fractured shell floating on a molten magma sea, punctured by new meteorite impacts or by the sinking of fragments as they became overly dense, scientists speculate. Until cooling made it possible for the crust to thicken and for plate tectonics to rework that crust into continental material, there would have been no continents to speak of.

But that's as far as agreements go. From here on, continental crust researchers part company.

Gradual crust proponents argue that at least five hundred million years passed before plate tectonics took hold and the continental crust began to build in pulses. It's the obvious conclusion, they say, since only silvers of continental crust in northern Canada and West Greenland, 3.96 billion years old and 3.8 billion years old respectively, date back that far. They reason that those must be examples of the first volcanic arcs that plate tectonics spawned and lumped together.

If older continents had existed, they would have eroded and perhaps left behind traces of themselves in the form of zircons—tough, gemlike nuggets of minerals which can become fused into new sedimentary rock without erasing their "memory" of when they formed. But Jonathan Patchett of the University of Arizona in Tucson analyzed zircons from the world's most ancient sedimentary rocks. With only a few exceptions, they hardly predated the 3.5- to 3.9-billion-year origins of the rocks themselves, he found. Although a few zircons found in western Australia date to 4.3 billion years ago, given their lack of company the gradual-crust camp regards them as freak occurrences.

Because more of the continental crust traces back to some periods of geological history than others, many gradual-growth advocates believe that the crust must have formed in bursts or episodes. They've proposed numerous timelines. For example, McLennan and S. Ross Taylor, a geochemist who recently retired from the Australian National University, say a surge in continent-making from roughly 3 billion to 2.5 billion years ago built half or more of the continental crust at once. That single pulse raised the continents to their average height of 2.75 miles above the seafloor, where they have remained to this day. Other, lesser, crust-forming episodes took place from 2 billion to 1.7 billion years ago and during later epochs.

An Early Start

Bowring and his "Big Bang" colleagues also think the Earth had a continental growth spurt. The difference is that they think it began almost as soon as the planet did.

As they see it, continent building would have started at the earliest possible moment—nearly at the planet's birth—and created the full continental volume in roughly a billion years. Then it would have settled into an equilibrium between continental crust formation and destruction that would linger for the rest of time. Why are there no vast outcrops from that stupendous outpouring of crust? It shows only that efficient continental crust-destruction forces gobbled them up, not that they never existed, they say.

This continental gobbling has only recently been accepted as a possibility. Crust is lighter than other parts of the planet, so mechanisms that could drag it back down again aren't immediately obvious. But recently some evidence of this "recycling" has popped to the surface. "There are lots of ways that crust can be returned to the mantle. I don't think that's a problem," says Bowring.

Terry Plank of the University of Kansas in Lawrence studies the fate of ocean sediments, much of which erode off the continents. She notes that independent estimates of the rate of sediment subduction—sediments getting dragged down into the mantle at ocean trenches—and the rate at which new crust builds are close: roughly one-third of a cubic mile per year apiece. "It is pretty remarkable that the two processes are in balance," she says.

It's not quite a cut-and-dried balance. Plank's own work indicates that as much as half of these sediments may belch right back up again from the mouths of volcanoes. But Bowring notes that continents may sacrifice themselves to the mantle in other ways. There is evidence, for instance, that the deep roots of mountain chains formed by continent collisions break off beneath those ranges. Other chunks can sink into the mantle at the boundaries of continents split by rifting, to name just two of a half-dozen circumstances, he says.

Even McLennan admits that the arguments for recycling have been persuasive, though not enough to win him over to the early burst idea. "Armstrong did convince us that you could indeed put this stuff back in," he says. Putting it in is, of course, different from specifying when "this stuff" came out, he's quick to add.

True, says Bowring. The evidence for the early appearance comes from someplace else. It comes from the chemistry of ancient igneous rocks, and ratios of trace rare-earth elements locked inside them. When mantle rock melts, as it must when crust is formed, certain elements tend to migrate into the rising material that will become the crust. One such element is neodymium. As a result, the mantle becomes relatively depleted in neodymium when some sort of crust separates out of it. The melting also enriches the continental rock that forms from this material.

Victoria Bennett, Allen Nutman, and Malcolm McCulloch of the Australian National University have measured ratios of neodymium to radioactive samarium, which decays to form neodymium, in formations dating from roughly 3.8 to 3.9 billion years ago in West Greenland. In rocks representative of the mantle of that period they found extraordinarily low amounts of neodymium in proportion to samarium. They are quick to say that it might be just a local pocket of depletion. But, if the rest of the mantle lost that much neodymium—and it would have been a lot—at that time, it would mean something quite remarkable. By 3.8 billion years ago, as much as one-and-a-third times the continental crust existing now might have already separated out of the mantle.

Comparing those findings to other ratios from ancient rocks in Labrador and northern Canada is encouraging, Bowring says. They also show strong signs of depletion, suggesting it indeed might have been a global phenomenon. What's more, the level of depletion stays about the same in much younger rocks. Thus, there was not the increasing depletion expected had there been gradual growth of new crust unaccompanied by recycling. On the other hand, some of the younger continental rocks were actually highly enriched in neodymium, a sign that they were formed out of much older continental rock that had previously separated out from the mantle below.

Tracing a Debate

In the face of those claims, Steven Moorbath and his colleagues at Oxford University in England threw down the gauntlet in an analysis published last year. The element ratios are not valid, they say, on the basis of their own study of neodymium ratios in rocks from the same formations. Their findings indicate that the rocks endured a period of metamorphism—that is, deformation and chemical change from pressure and heat—and probably even melted around 3.37 billion years ago, skewing their element ratios.

Early-burst advocates dismiss Moorbath's claims. They also note that studies of other elements—uranium and niobium—done by Paul Sylvester and his colleagues at Australian National University are also producing ratios favorable to an early crust, although these results come from different and younger rock formations.

But Moorbath is not the only one shouting at the elements. A separate analysis by Arizona's Patchett and Jeff Vervoort, who focused on yet another element, hafnium, has also cast doubt on West Greenland data, although it also suggests that some continental crust had already formed by 3.8 billion years ago.

At a meeting last June on continental crust origins, the controversy boiled over into a public clash. It happened as Victoria Bennett ended a talk explaining why the hafnium ratios left her extreme-depletion conclusions intact. Such dry details do not ordinarily provoke protesters to jump to their feet. Yet this did. From the audience, Moorbath stood up, along with other scientists, to air his conclusions, which Bennett had not mentioned. Another researcher then demanded, to a smattering of applause, that Bennett admit she was wrong. "Certainly that sort of attack was unpleasant," Bennett says, "but the attack was a shouting match, not a rebuttal of ideas on a scientific basis." Bennett argued heatedly for her point of view. She would have had more allies, noted another scientist present at the meeting, except that the conference had attracted more of the gradual growth crowd.

There may be a lesson emerging from the fracas, says Donald Depaolo, a geochemist at the University of California in Berkeley, who helped establish the samarium-neodymium technique and who favors the early-burst view. He's been worried that the controversial ratios meant something was wrong with the basis of the technique, and plans to test a series of rocks from the same regions in his lab. "In most cases, whenever you get down to debating it means you don't understand what's going on. This is science and someone has to take it to the next level."

Reproduced with permission from Peter Weiss.

Earth's moon is so large that Earth and its satellite are sometimes referred to as a "double planet." Prior to the Apollo missions, there was no single convincing theory about how the Moon was formed. Nonetheless, soil and rock samples brought back from the Moon indicate that Earth and the Moon are closely related. This has been ascertained because these samples show that the Moon and Earth were formed in the same general region of the solar system. However, the Moon's density resembles that of Earth's mantle (the rocky portion of Earth's surface that's sandwiched between the dense core and the light outer crust) rather than Earth's overall average density. This means that the Moon's composition is similar to what is only a secondary feature of our planet. Why is this so?

The idea that, at one time, the Moon was covered with a molten magma ocean that resulted in the formation of the crust has been proposed. But there are difficulties with this theory because of the problem of accounting for the heat source that is responsible for the molten sea. The author uses the history of bombardment of the early Earth and Moon to address this question and explain their present development. They propose a provocative model in which the present-day state of the Earth and Moon results from the collision of an earlier pair of double planets that formed at the same site.—EF

"How Earth Got Its Moon"
by Paul D. Spudis
Astronomy, July 2004

Abstract: Many people think of Earth and its Moon as a double planet, but the pair strikes scientists more as an odd couple. Even the "double" part, they've found, is oddly ironic.

To judge by its nearest neighbors, the Earth-Moon system is different—you could even call it strange. Venus, a nearby rocky planet, revolves around the Sun alone; no moon brightens its cloudtops. Mars has two little rock-like satellites, Phobos and Deimos, but each is smaller in size than the craters visible in the smallest telescopic views of our Moon. And then there's Mercury, with a cratered surface that looks like a big Moon, while its inside resembles a little Earth with an enormous iron core. But just like Venus, Mercury travels alone and moonless.

Yes, something about our corner of the solar system looks different. Earth has a moon and it's huge, relatively speaking. The words double planet, often used to characterize Earth and the Moon, make an interesting term, one that embodies an ironic truth.

In the years before and immediately after the Apollo missions, no single idea for the Moon's origin was accepted by scientists. The three traditional models of lunar origin all were thought to be flawed in one sense or another. The "capture" model held that the Moon formed elsewhere and was snagged into Earth's orbit during a glancing, near-miss encounter. The "fission" model suggested the Moon was ripped out of Earth's body, splitting into a double-planet system like a reproducing amoebic cell. The "co-accretion" model theorized Earth and the Moon formed in the same part of the solar system but as separate planets, independent of each other before joining gravitationally.

Some hard facts about the Moon were known before we went there, but no idea fully fit its observed properties and inferred history. For example, the Moon's average density is much lower than Earth's—3.3 times that of water compared to Earth's 5.5 times. However, the lunar density comes close to the density of Earth's mantle, the rocky portion sandwiched between the light outer crust and the dense inner core.

The Apollo missions proved that Earth and the Moon are closely related—oxygen isotopes of lunar samples show the Moon formed in the same general region of the solar system as Earth. The samples also indicate the Moon has a low content of volatile elements, suggesting its birth involved high temperatures that would have destroyed such elements. What struck scientists as weird, however, was that while the Moon's chemistry most closely resembles Earth's mantle, the mantle is a secondary feature of our planet's evolution. It emerged when Earth, soon after formation, differentiated into mantle and core. How could any kind of moon, born as an independent body, have a composition matching the mantle?

Scientists tend to solve their knottiest problems while working on ones believed to be totally different. Some key clues to the origin of the Moon involved evidence from two, seemingly unrelated, problems: the origin of small, white pebbles in the dark soil of the Apollo 11 landing site, and the mapping and measurement of ancient impact basins on the Moon.

White Stones

Small fragments of white rocks contained in the soil collected and returned by the Apollo 11 astronauts suggested the highlands (the bright, rugged uplands of the Moon) are made of an igneous rock type called anorthosite. This rock cooled from an initially molten state and consists almost entirely of the light-toned, low-density mineral plagioclase feldspar.

Making rocks composed of a single mineral is not easy because nature tends to mix things. In this case, the difficulty is compounded by the fact that no known kind of magma (molten rock) has a composition corresponding to anorthosite. Worse was the sheer quantity of anorthosite found on the Moon. From the Apollo data, it was evident that anorthosite and similar rock types make up much of the lunar crust. That's a lot of rock to explain.

The solution lies in the low density of plagioclase compared to other common lunar minerals. A Moon encircled by an ocean of liquid rock would soon develop a film on its surface—a skin of plagioclase crystals floating on a magma made of the lunar bulk composition. As this magma ocean cooled, the film thickened into the rock anorthosite, creating a plagioclase-rich upper crust. Similarly, the high-density, iron- and magnesium-rich minerals olivine and pyroxene sank, accumulating at the bottom of the magma ocean. Thus, the magma ocean solidified from two directions, thickening downward as the anorthositic crust grew, and building upward as olivine and pyroxene crystals settled to the bottom of the sea of molten rock to form the lunar mantle.

This basic story was reasonably well understood shortly after the Apollo program ended in the early 1970s. However, questions lingered about the source of heat that created the magma ocean in the first place. A very rapid pace of accretion could help answer that question. But was such a fast pace possible when all existing studies indicated the planets took a considerable time to accrete? The problem of accounting for the magma ocean's heat source caused some investigators to abandon the idea altogether. Then came some new thinking about the bombardment history of the early planets.

Biggest Basin

At the time the magma ocean existed, Earth and the Moon were coalescing out of debris left over from planetary formation. In the Moon's case, we can still see a record of the tail end of this early bombardment with even a small telescope: the rough, heavily cratered face of the ancient highlands. Geologic mapping done to support the Apollo missions led planetary scientists to recognize that craters exist in a continuous spectrum of size from microscopic to thousands of miles across. Detailed mapping, however, showed the largest crater appeared to be on the Moon's farside. But the structure was glimpsed only briefly from orbiting Apollo spacecraft (and poorly photographed), so its size and nature remained vague.

The feature was named the South Pole-Aitken basin (SPA) from two unrelated, superimposed features. It appears noticeably darker than the rest of the generally bright farside. In 1990, pictures returned by the Galileo spacecraft revealed the basin has a distinct composition, while its dark appearance suggests the basin floor is made of rocks rich in iron. In fact, scientists eventually concluded the floor might be the lower crust of the Moon, exposed after a gigantic impact stripped off the anorthosite-rich upper crust.

In 1994, the Clementine spacecraft's laser altimeter made a global topographic map of the Moon, revealing the basin's true nature and extent. It spans more than 1,500 miles (2,500 km)—the distance between Houston and Los Angeles—and ranges from 5 to 8 miles (8 to 13 km) deep. SPA is the oldest surviving impact basin on the Moon. Mineralogical mapping by Clementine (and the Lunar Prospector spacecraft a few years later) showed that SPA has a composition unmatched anywhere else on the Moon.

The discovery of this feature was a key piece of evidence in the search for the Moon's origin. The basin's large size shows that big, planetary-scale collisions actually occurred. Such impacts had scarcely been imagined, let alone modeled scientifically. Yet subsequently, many computer simulations have shown possible outlines for the origin of the Moon.

$$1 + 1 = 1 + 1?$$

Planetary scientists now believe that 4.6 billion years ago, at least two planets existed in the space now inhabited by Earth. One was a protoplanet about the size of Mars, while the other was a proto-Earth, with 50 to 90 percent its present size and mass.

The model works best when the proto-impactor hits Earth with an oblique blow that reinforces its existing spin. Such a collision would have several effects. First, the off-center hit speeds up Earth's rotation. Second, the mantles of both impactor and proto-Earth are vaporized by the energy of the impact. Third, most of the impactor's mass bounces off the proto-Earth; it flies in a ballistic path that brings it back to reaccrete onto Earth's surface sometime later. Finally, a quantity of vaporized debris, mostly from the mantle of the proto-impactor (with some proto-Earth mantle as well), shoots into orbit around Earth. This white-hot material cools very quickly, turning into a disk of fine debris. In the giant impact's immediate aftermath, Earth resembled a chaotic Saturn, at least for a time.

Such a disk has no stability, however. After the loose particles migrate outside the point where tidal stresses prevent them from coalescing, they accrete quickly into a moon. Estimates of the accretion time scale range from a few to several thousand years, very rapid in geological terms. The energy of accretion appears as heat that cannot easily dissipate—and the result is a body that melted almost totally.

Still, details of the Moon's assembly remain imperfectly understood. Did it occur all at once, as a myriad of small objects combined into a fully formed Moon, or did a group of smaller submoons form first and then smash together? The Moon has several global asymmetries. For example, the nearside and farside differ in how much mare they possess, and the eastern and western halves of the nearside show compositional differences. Perhaps these variations reflect an early series of large impacts, each being the merger of many sub-moons into a growing, rapidly evolving new planet that we might call Luna.

Double Planet

Therefore, the old adage about Earth and the Moon being a double planet masks a subtle irony. Yes, they are a double planet—but they are the second double planet to orbit here. After the first two collided in a giant impact, a new planetary pair formed—Terra and Luna. These two worlds, each with its own fascinating history and evolution, are closely linked by a deep-seated planetary kinship. Our geologically active Earth has erased most clues of its very early history. But the story of our system's violent birth, global melting, and impacts of unimaginable intensity is coming to light as scientists study lunar rocks and global maps of the Moon.

Separated at birth but reunited by chance, these two worlds dance together across the solar system. The original two worlds that collided here 4.6 billion years ago no longer exist. They merged, forming a unique system—a pair of bodies no longer orbiting the Sun independently, but a true double planet, bound together by gravity, history, and geochemistry.

Simulating a Giant Impact

Smashing planets together in a computer allows scientists to construct a likely scenario for the origin of the Moon and Earth. A Mars-size impactor hits the proto-Earth a glancing blow, shooting debris into orbit. This later coalesces into the Moon. In the simulation, colors show the temperature range. Medium blue is 2,000 kelvins (3,600 [degrees] Fahrenheit), while red is 7,000 kelvins (13,000 [degrees] F). The final frame (see page 47 in original article) shows the Earth-Moon system edge-on.

Reproduced by permission. © 2004 *Astronomy* magazine, Kalmbach Publishing Co.

The idea that large meteorite impacts can cause volcanic eruptions on Earth's surface is

considered to be quite controversial. Nonetheless, new evidence has been discovered that supports this theory.

Dallas Abbott of Columbia University and Ann Isley from the State University of New York have been studying the time of thirty-eight meteorite impacts. Their findings indicate that the meteorite impacts correlate with volcanic eruptions. Such large meteorites may have broken through Earth's crust, causing eruptions and, at the same time, leaving no evidence of their passing because they sank beneath the crust and were covered by the resultant lava flow.

According to the author, given the number of meteors in the sky, one would expect Earth to have been hit 440 times by large asteroids in the past 250 million years. But only thirty-eight such craters have been identified by scientists. The theory proposed by Abbott and Isley could account for this discrepancy. Their theory and the views of other astronomers on it are discussed in the following article.—EF

"Did Lava Cover Traces of Asteroid Impacts?"
by Kate Ravilious
New Scientist, December 14, 2002

Gigantic meteorites could have crashed straight through the Earth's crust leaving no sign of a crater.

As if gouging a huge crater and throwing up vast dust clouds wasn't bad enough, large meteorite impacts may punch right through the Earth's crust, triggering gigantic volcanic eruptions.

The idea is controversial, but evidence is mounting that the Earth's geology has largely been driven by such events. This would also explain why our planet has so few impact crater remnants. Counting the number of asteroids we see in the sky suggests that over the past 250 million years, Earth should have been hit around 440 times by asteroids larger than one kilometre across. But scientists have found only 38 large impact craters from this period.

Dallas Abbott from Columbia University and her colleague Ann Isley from the State University of New York studied the timing of these 38 impacts and found that they correlate strongly with eruptions of "mantle-plume" volcanoes during the same period. Most volcanoes come from small amounts of the Earth's upper mantle boiling over, but mantle-plume volcanoes happen when hot rock from deep within the Earth's mantle shoots straight up through the Earth's crust. The timing suggests that these volcanoes are related to asteroid impacts, Abbott and Isley report in Earth and Planetary Science Letters (vol 205, p 53).

Not everyone agrees. "I am not enthusiastic about the idea that impacts systematically control Earth's activity," says Boris Ivanov from the Institute of Geospheres Dynamics in Moscow. He has used computer models to investigate the effect of meteorites on the Earth's crust, and says he doesn't believe impacts are capable of having a significant effect on the planet's geological processes. And geochemist Christian Koeberl from Vienna University argues that the dates Abbott used are not reliable. "The impacts and volcanoes can only be correlated to within tens of millions of years," he says. "This doesn't really prove anything."

But elsewhere, there is growing support for the idea that Earth's volcanism may be closely entwined with meteorite impacts. Adrian Jones and David Price from University College London say Abbott's work backs up their recent computer simulations. These models suggest meteorites bigger than about 10 kilometres across could sometimes punch right through the Earth's crust, causing huge volcanic eruptions (Earth and Planetary Science Letters, vol 202, p 551). "A large impact has the ability to cause instant melting where it hits, creating its own impact plume in the mantle and resulting in a massive surge of lava spilling out," Jones explains.

Until now Abbott and Isley weren't sure how impacts might trigger volcanic eruptions, but the UCL model suggests a mechanism. It would also explain why we don't see as many meteorite craters as we might expect, as the surges of molten rock would obliterate them.

Jones speculates that many of the impact craters Abbott analysed could have been created by mere fragments of bigger asteroids that hit elsewhere at the same time and broke through the crust, ultimately leaving no trace. For example, the 10 kilometre-wide asteroid that hit Chicxulub in Mexico 65 million years ago is widely blamed for wiping out the dinosaurs. But it could have been a piece from a much bigger rock that hit India, triggering the surge of volcanic activity known as the Deccan Traps.

"Many areas that exhibit extensive volcanism from the past, such as the Deccan Traps and the Siberian Traps, may in fact be sites of gigantic meteorite impacts," says Jones. Perhaps the dinosaurs would have survived a meteorite impact alone, but the double whammy of a meteorite and volcanoes pushed them to extinction.

Reprinted with permission from *New Scientist*.

A layer of dense cloud cover obscures the surface of Venus. This keeps us from viewing it through conventional devices such as telescopes. Scientists have long been fascinated by Venus because its size and mass are so similar to that of Earth.

Although we have not been able to view Venus's surface directly, it has been possible to use X-rays to get a sense of what Venus's surface is like. In the 1970s and 1980s, Soviet and American spacecraft were able to generate rudimentary X-ray maps of Venus's surface. Then, in the early 1990s, the Magellan radar mapper began to orbit Venus. As a result, it was possible to get an idea of what the cratered surface of Venus looked like for the first time. The nature of these craters reveal some interesting information about the age of Earth's neighboring planet. The craters also provide valuable clues as to how Venus was formed.—EF

"Venus Unveiled: A Great Volcanic Flood Must Have Resurfaced Earth's Sister World Some 600 Million Years Ago"
by David H. Grinspoon
Astronomy, May 1997

Abstract: The Magellan radar mappers of the 1990s have greatly expanded the surface detail to be seen on Venus. The cloud cover will not allow visible light to penetrate, but radar is able to pass through easily. About 98% of the planet's surface has been mapped. Its surface has been shaped by volcanos.

No human eye has ever gazed on the surface of Venus. A thick overcast of impenetrable clouds hides the surface from view. For planetary scientists trying to piece together the planet's history, this poses a distinct problem: Impact craters are the prime chronicle of that history, but if the craters can't be seen, they can't be interpreted either. Because the size and mass of Venus closely match those of Earth, many scientists speculated that the two also had similar histories.

Fortunately, although the venusian clouds are opaque to visible light, radar easily penetrates them. In the 1970s and '80s, the Soviet Venera and American Pioneer spacecraft made coarse radar maps of Venus's surface. But it wasn't until the early 1990s, when the sophisticated Magellan radar mapper went into orbit around Venus, that scientists could clearly see impact craters. Once Magellan had mapped most of the surface, planetary scientists could study the global distribution of craters and look for clues to the planet's history.

In rural areas of the United States, where guns are commonplace and youth are bored, you can roughly date road signs by the number of bullet holes found in them. The older signs are more shot up. It's the same with craters and planetary surfaces. Impact craters are found nearly everywhere in the solar system; they are the universal chronometers of planetary science. In the absence of other processes, a planet will gradually accumulate craters from the random impacts of asteroids and comets. Astronomers know fairly well how many of these stray bodies exist and how often they hit planets, so crater density can be used to calculate the age of a surface. In Magellan images of Venus, just over 900 impact craters have been counted, which corresponds to an average age of half a billion years, give or take a couple of hundred million. This makes it by far the youngest planetary surface in the inner solar system, except for Earth's.

Comparing the crater density in different areas and different types of terrain helps planetary scientists assemble a historical sequence for a planet. Older, less active areas will have collected more craters, while craters have been wiped out on younger, more active surfaces. For example, the relatively young northern plains of Mars are much more sparsely cratered than the ancient southern highlands. This technique works great on most rocky planets. It has helped us learn the history of Mars and the moon. But it doesn't work on Venus.

Venus is "impact challenged." Its surface lacks small craters. It's easy to see why if you imagine standing in a few inches of water and throwing rocks of different sizes down at the sand beneath the water. With pebbles, you can't make a dent in the sand below because the water slows them down and they fall gently to the bottom. A large boulder that you can barely lift will make a nice little crater because the water can't stop it. Now if you change the depth of water, you change the critical size between rocks that can and cannot make craters. The more water, the bigger the rock you need. Similarly, the thicker a planet's atmosphere the larger an incoming object has to be to survive its high velocity passage through the air and make a crater. Every planet that has an atmosphere has a cutoff size, depending on the atmosphere's thickness, below which there are no craters on the surface.

On Venus, the smaller impacting objects that would otherwise do most of the cratering are filtered out by the thick atmosphere. They burn up or explode before they hit the ground, just like meteors do on Earth. On Earth, only dust and pebbles get snuffed (making "shooting stars"), but on Venus you don't get any craters smaller than about two miles across.

Any well-cratered planetary surface has many more small craters than big ones, because there are many more small stray objects in space than big ones. Although these holes are rather small, we have to count them all. The overall peppering of Mars and the moon with very small craters is what allows planetary scientists to determine the relative ages of different areas. But because Venus has no small craters, they can't help determine the planet's chronology. All areas have more or less the same small number of craters. Although some minor variations in crater density exist from place to place, these are of the kind that we would expect to be produced by the blind marksman of impact cratering. A global map of craters on Venus is indistinguishable from a random pattern.

It turns out to be tough to reconstruct a history for Venus, at least using images taken from orbit. Many of the usual techniques just don't work. Crater counting is out, and erosion is pretty much useless because basically nothing is eroded. (On Mars older features are noticeably more heavily sandblasted by wind and buried by dust than younger ones.) So planetary scientists must rely on other means to assemble a chronology of the surface. In some places it is obvious, on a local scale, that a particular flow or episode of faulting came earlier or later, but efforts to construct a global history have been controversial. For example, it is clear in individual locales that the tesserae—rugged, deformed highland mountains—predate the smooth plains, which lap up onto them. But does this mean that *all* tesserae are older than *all* plains, everywhere around the planet? On any other planet we could just count craters and find the answer. On Venus, we must coax the answers from more subtle clues.

There's another reason why the history of the venusian surface has been tricky to decipher. The first clues to this bizarre history came when planetary scientists noticed that something is not quite right about the impact craters.

What's Eating the Craters of Venus?

All the craters on Venus look unnaturally pristine. Instead of blending into the volcanic plains that cover most of the planet, they seem planted on top as an afterthought, as though a crew had built a cheap movie-set planet and realized at the last minute that they had better throw in some craters.

The total number of craters indicates that the planet's surface is not very old by planetary standards—a billion years, tops. Therefore, some process has removed most of the craters that ever formed on the planet. But there are *no signs* of any such process. The thief who stole Venus's craters has successfully covered his tracks. There are three suspects, but each has a good defense.

If *erosion* were the culprit, we would see a broad range of craters, from pristine fresh ones to highly degraded ones that have nearly disappeared. That's the case on Mars, where erosion by windblown dust is a dominant process.

Craters can also be destroyed by tectonic disruption, if they are simply cracked and faulted to the point where they are no longer recognizable. Here again, we would expect to see the process at work, but Venus shows few partially disrupted craters.

A prime suspect is *volcanism*, because volcanic flows dominate the surface. But if craters were being covered by lava, then lots of them should be partially buried beneath the plains. On the moon, for example, the volcanic plains contain craters ranging from those with barely detectable circular outlines that have been almost completely covered by lava to those that are almost pristine but have lava flows lapping slightly up their flanks. On Venus only about 4 percent of the craters are partially covered by volcanic flows, and almost none are mostly buried. This seems to rule out volcanism as a dominant process removing craters. Why, on a planet smothered with volcanic features, are the craters so untouched? Do volcanos on Venus worship craters, as Hindus venerate cows, and thus spare them from their otherwise global carnage? This is not a favored hypothesis, but there has to be a way to explain the odd, and globally pervasive, occurrence of pristine craters overlaying widespread lava plains.

It is as if some mysterious process were swallowing craters whole and leaving no trace. There are a few ways this appearance could come about. If you see a road sign full of holes, it is not necessarily old. Some well-armed fool pumped up on testosterone and booze could have opened fire on it the night before last. What if all the craters really were added as a kind of afterthought, produced by a very recent barrage of impacts? On any planet with reasonable erosion rates, you could test this idea by noticing if some of the craters were worn down, showing signs of age. (Are the bullet holes rusted?) But with little erosion on Venus, you can't tell, so the hypothesis is consistent with the way all the craters sit atop the "paint job" of planetwide lava flows.

Unfortunately, this scenario ranks as only slightly more plausible than crater-worshipping volcanos.

Everything we know about the inner solar system suggests that there has been no recent burst of cratering activity. Impacting objects do not discriminate greatly among the terrestrial planets. If there had been a recent shower of large meteoroids, we would also see its effects on the surfaces of the moon, Mars, and Earth. We don't.

One scientist suggested that Venus could have had a moon that disintegrated relatively recently, showering the planet with fragments that made most of the craters. Although this theory is hard to disprove, it remains unsatisfying. Scientists don't like to resort to explanations that require extraordinary or fortuitously timed events unless all other possibilities have been exhausted. You can always invent a contrived theory to explain any observation, but the universe in general does not seem designed like a Rube Goldberg machine, and if we dig deeper we can often find simplicity. This preference for simplicity is called Ockham's razor.

Venus Gets a Complete Makeover

Here is another way to explain the unusual crater population—Suppose that half a billion years ago something suddenly happened to Venus, wiping out all older craters. Vast lava flows occurring simultaneously all over the planet would do the trick. Then, if there has been relatively little surface activity since that time and Venus has been slowly collecting craters all along, things should look as they do.

This idea, called catastrophic resurfacing, rubs many scientists the wrong way. Like the disrupted moon theory, it invokes a special event, and quite an incredible one at that. We can hear Ockham sharpening his razor. Some scientists would prefer a steady-state model—one that employs ongoing processes operating at more or less constant rates and that does not require a fundamental change in the planet during the geologically recent past. Many vigorous arguments have been offered in valiant attempts to save us from having to accept catastrophe. Perhaps craters have been steadily destroyed all along by volcanic and tectonic disruptions that are just the right size to destroy whole craters but not partial ones. If small patches of the surface are continually destroyed in this way, eventually the whole surface will be affected and no traces of older craters will be left.

To test these competing ideas, planetary scientists have developed new computer models that simulate the evolution of the surface of Venus. The results have confirmed what seems intuitively correct: If craters are forming at random and are being destroyed by volcanism (which is also randomly occurring over a long period of time), then a lot more craters should be partially covered by lava flows. To return to the bullet-holes-in-road-sign analogy, if someone is going around repainting signs that have been shot up, then holes that have been painted on should be common. If not, the painting must have stopped before most of the shooting. These models seem to support the catastrophic resurfacing theory.

The initially disturbing idea of catastrophic resurfacing became more palatable when it received support from other lines of reasoning. Models of the interior evolution of Venus suggest that the planet oscillates between periods of relative quiescence and periods of instability and rapid surface overturn. In other words, Venus may "freak out" occasionally, getting rid of its internal heat in great planetwide spasms of activity, rather than in the steadier cycling of lithospheric plates that occurs on Earth. These models predict intermittent bursts of greatly enhanced volcanic activity at intervals of several hundred million years. If this scenario is true, the observed crater population could simply reflect the accumulation of impacts since the last time Venus turned inside out.

The initial proposal of the catastrophic resurfacing model drew strong reactions, for and against, from many planetary scientists. Several years of frustrating debates had two sides repeating the same arguments, and it wasn't clear that anyone was listening. Perhaps the community became briefly stuck in this cul-de-sac because of the power of the loaded word catastrophic. It recalls the conflict between *catastrophic* and uniformitarian views of Earth history. Geologists have spent much of the last several centuries demonstrating that surface features on Earth can be explained without recourse to a biblical flood. Must we now accept that much of Venus's surface was created in one great volcanic flood of similar proportions? The search for a steady-state model to explain the craters of Venus can be seen as an attempt to find a uniformitarian alternative. Perhaps the choice of the phrase "catastrophic resurfacing" was unfortunate, and "sudden global resurfacing" would have provoked a more constructive debate (although it does not sound as scientific).

The repetitive debate seems to have largely died down, to the great relief of most Venus scientists. Although some controversy continues, the community seems to be converging toward an acceptance of something like catastrophic resurfacing (although not everyone calls it that). Roughly 600 million years ago, Venus seems to have been wiped clean of craters. Some combination of widespread volcanic flooding and tectonic disruption created a tabula rasa for later cratering. Most of this activity died down quickly, producing a planetary surface that may be nearly all the same age. But planets are never this simple. Even if Venus did receive a near-complete makeover 600 million years ago, any complete picture must include the greater complexity inevitable in an Earth-sized planet.

A lower rate of volcanism and tectonic activity has continued in certain areas to the present day, producing the small number of flooded and disrupted craters. Several lines of evidence support this, including fresh flows on some volcanos, particularly the large shield volcanos (although the lack of erosion *could* fool us into thinking older flows are fresh), and the nonequilibrium mix of atmospheric gases, with an excess of sulfur dioxide probably supplied by active volcanos.

Newer, more detailed analysis of the global crater distribution also points toward more recent surface activity. Although no large areas of lower or higher crater density can be found, some *types* of terrain have more craters than others. For example, the large volcanos have fewer craters than other areas: they seem to be, on average, only half the age of the global plains. The highly deformed tesserae are apparently the oldest areas of Venus. They may be the only remnants of the surface that existed *before* catastrophic resurfacing—high-altitude "islands" that escaped the global volcanic flooding. If so, then perhaps they should have more craters than other areas. This is hard to prove, however, possibly because craters are hard to pick out on images of these highly cracked and wrinkled surfaces. Compared with the smooth plains, searching for craters on the tesserae is like playing "Where's Waldo on Venus?" Many distracting details make it hard to find what you are looking for.

Venus seems to have changed not only its rate of volcanism but its style, fairly abruptly, around 600 million years ago. Before then the planet was vigorously repaving itself with vast plains of basalt. Then, for reasons we don't understand but that must be related to the evolving interior of the planet, it switched over to a lower rate of volcanism, concentrated in specific areas where hot spots forced up broad domes in the lithosphere, creating giant shield volcanos.

If this general picture holds up, the implications for the evolution of Venus are staggering. To cover up all preexisting craters, an episode of rapid volcanism would have had to flood most of the planet's surface with lava to a depth of three to six miles. This implies a rate of volcanism 50 to 1,000 times higher than the recent rate, depending on how long the activity lasted.

Once again planetary scientists are forced to accept that some aspects of planetary evolution have been anything but uniformitarian. Our recently increased appreciation for the role of large impacts in planetary origins and evolution should make this easier to swallow. But large impacts are outside invaders, whatever wiped out the surface of Venus came from within.

Unfortunately, there was no one around to see what Venus looked like during the great flood. But with the detailed views provided by Magellan and the ingenuity of planetary scientists, we can be confident that it did occur.

Reproduced with permission from David H. Grinspoon.

Venus is Earth's nearest neighbor; it's the planet closest to Earth in terms of size as well as being the most visible in the night sky. However, because of its dense cloud cover and the incredible temperatures on its surface, scientists have had little hope of finding life there. Therefore, Venus has never received the amount of attention that Mars has.

A few planetary scientists are beginning to rethink this situation. These scientists believe that Venus's lack of large bodies of water might not be a barrier to life. The following article, "Don't Ignore the Planet Next Door," discusses the changes that may have taken place over time on

Venus's surface, the nature of the planet and its physical composition and atmosphere, and the rationale for thinking that life may be possible even in such an inhospitable environment.—EF

"Don't Ignore the Planet Next Door"
by Oliver Morton
***Science*, November 29, 2002**

Is it time for a closer look at Venus? Some researchers say life could exist in its veil of clouds, and it could help us understand planets around distant stars.

London—Venus is the planet nearest to Earth, closest to Earth in size, and the brightest in Earth's skies. As such it would seem hard to overlook, yet overlooked it is. While NASA and the world's other space agencies lavish money on Mars—dispatching probes at an average of more than one per year—and eye other planetary prospects farther afield, such as Jupiter's moon Europa, they hardly spare a thought for Venus. The reason is water. Although Mars might look like a parched and frozen desert, its surface was marked by water in the distant past, and water may persist at some depth today. Water, the logic goes, means the possibility of life, in the past if not the present. Water thus makes a planet interesting. And water is something that Venus—with an average surface temperature of 460 [degrees] C—conspicuously lacks.

Although inhospitable, Venus is not completely ignored. The European Space Agency (ESA) this month approved Venus Express—a mission to study the planet's atmosphere—for launch in 2005. But it's a cut-price project, cobbled together using instruments from ESA's Mars Express and Rosetta missions and built around a copy of the Mars Express spacecraft; it is not custom built for studying Venus. And even this modest effort was nearly cancelled earlier in the year because of budget problems.

Although Japan plans to launch a small satellite to study the atmosphere in 2007 or later, there is no major commitment to ongoing studies of Venus in any of the world's space agencies. NASA will have launched its first mission to look for Earth-sized planets around other stars well before it next sends a spacecraft to the Earth-sized planet next door. As Kevin Baines, a planetary scientist at NASA's Jet Propulsion Laboratory (JPL) in Pasadena, California, puts it, "There is little hope of finding life or signs of ancient life. So, Venus always seems to fall to the bottom of the list."

But not all of his colleagues accept Baines's premise. A few planetary scientists are starting to think it might be wrong to assume that Venus is a hopeless prospect for finding life. Their optimism stems not from any new information about Venus but from looking at what is known in a different way. Although it clearly lacks any extensive bodies of liquid water, Venus might still be conducive to life, they argue. Indeed, according to David Grinspoon, a planetary scientist at the Southwest Research Institute in Boulder, Colorado, Venus is as good a place to look for life today as either Europa or

Mars—maybe better. "The case for possible life there is really as strong as on any other planet," says Grinspoon.

So far, Grinspoon and his fellow Venus devotees haven't won over many of their colleagues. One eminent astrobiologist muses that it's interesting that a science which until very recently was viewed as on the fringe should now have a fringe of its own. But researchers in that fringe have started publishing papers and presenting ideas at conferences about both life on Venus and ways to study it. And if they haven't convinced many that Venus might harbor life, they have another argument that seems more compelling: We should be taking a closer look at Venus in order to prepare for what we might find when we look for life around other stars.

Grinspoon first started thinking about life on Venus in the mid-1990s. While writing the conclusion to a book about Venus, he tried to put together a case for life on the planet, just to see if such a case could be made. "My devil's advocate case was good enough to convince me, not that there is life there, but that there could be," he says.

The argument begins by noting that Venus might well have been as good a habitat for life as Earth or Mars were when the solar system was young; most opinion has it much cooler then than it is today, with every chance of liquid water. If Venus did not offer the right conditions for the origin of life—whatever they may be—it would still have provided a welcoming and clement landfall for any microbes on meteorites knocked off Earth or Mars. The chances of life on an early Venus are thus not that different from the chances of life on Mars at roughly the same time.

Unfortunately, both planets then under went quite vicious changes of climate. On Mars, what surface water there might have been froze. Life would have been forced underground, where the planet's warmth would allow liquid water to cling on in deep aquifers and hydrothermal systems. It might persist there to this day. On Venus the problem was not the cold but the heat: a runaway greenhouse effect that boiled away the surface water. Grinspoon reasons that life on Venus, faced with the opposite problem of life on Mars, might have hit upon the opposite solution: migrating up into the sky to keep cool rather than down into the ground to keep warm.

Compared to its surface, the skies of Venus look positively alluring. The atmosphere contains some water vapor—although only a very little—and its clouds are at a sufficient height for that water to condense out in liquid form. Some of the cloud droplets at these altitudes are larger than the droplets in clouds above Earth are and thus are more than large enough to contain microbes. The clouds are continuous and permanent, and the individual cloud droplets stay aloft for months, so they could provide a reasonably stable environment. Thanks to presumed continuing volcanism, the clouds exist in an atmosphere rich in chemicals that living organisms might use to fuel their metabolisms, and there is plenty of sunlight for photosynthesis. Admittedly, the cloud droplets are composed of very highly concentrated sulfuric acid, and this might appear to be a showstopper. But microbes can survive in some very unlikely surroundings.

Indeed, since Grinspoon first started to advocate it, his devilish case for life above the hellish surface of Venus has received circumstantial support from studies of life on Earth. Earthly bacteria have been discovered in ever more acidic environments; some have now been found that thrive at pH levels as low as 0. And although it had long been thought that the only bacteria in cloud droplets were inert spores or were in suspended animation, recent measurements made in the Alps have shown that the bacteria in clouds can be metabolically active. If some earthly microbes can live in clouds and others in strong sulfuric acid, why shouldn't microbes on Venus have learned to do both at once?

In some ways, says microbiologist Dirk Schulze-Makuch of the University of Texas, El Paso, the permanent cloud cover of Venus might actually make a better home for microbes than the short-lived clouds of Earth. One possible energy source that venusian microbes might use, he speculates, is ultraviolet light. For decades, it has been known that there is something in the clouds over Venus that absorbs UV light very well. As yet, no one knows what it is—an organic pigment, perhaps?

Charles Cockell, a microbiologist at the British Antarctic Survey in Cambridge who wrote a paper about the astrobiological potential of Venus in 1999, is one of many who hold out little hope for such ideas of life in the clouds. Sulfuric acid is a powerful desiccating agent, and acid as strong as that in Venus's cloud droplets, he says, would pull the water straight out of any cells immersed in it. David Crisp of JPL, who chaired a panel that provided ideas about Venus to the recent decadal survey of planetary science done by the U.S. National Research Council, agrees. "[Schulze-Makuch and his co-author] make the assumption that there are water droplets, but that's fundamentally incorrect, as far as we know. There's no evidence for liquid water on Venus that's not bound in very, very concentrated solutions of sulfuric acid: 75% to 85% pure sulfuric acid."

Grinspoon does not accept that there is no overlap between the range of pH values earthly microbes can tolerate and the range found in the clouds of Venus. But even if the clouds of Venus are too acidic for any Earth-like life, that does not rule out life of other sorts. Steven Benner, a biochemist at the University of Florida, Gainesville, points out that the idea that water is necessary for life is far from proven. Some chemical reactions that might be the basis of different forms of life take place best under conditions where water is excluded, such as those of superacidity. And Benner thinks that if we can't imagine life existing in the clouds, that might just show our lack of imagination.

However plausible the case for life in the clouds of Venus is, it will be difficult to test. Bringing a sample of Venus's clouds back to Earth sounds quite simple: Design a probe to dip into the atmosphere as it flies by the planet, scoop up a bit of its surroundings, and carry on along a trajectory that brings it back to Earth. A mixture of aerobraking techniques like those used by Mars probes and sampling canisters like those on the Stardust mission to sample cometary dust would do the trick.

But Grinspoon worries that gathering up a sample at such speed might smash the very things that are being sought. And Crisp points out that designing a sample-return canister that can bring powerful and poorly characterized acids back to Earth in a pristine form is no easy task. Even if you could bring a sample back, looking for life in it would require a secure containment facility here on Earth. If the laboratory slated for dealing with the samples to be returned from Mars were used, then that cost could be avoided, but that laboratory is more than 10 years off.

Attempts to sample the atmosphere are hampered by the lack of a thorough understanding of how the planet works. Although more than 20 spacecraft from the United States and the Soviet Union visited Venus in the 1960s, 1970s, and 1980s, big questions—such as how its atmosphere works, what its surface is like, and how the two interact—still have not been answered. Crisp argues that this lack of understanding has led to the belief that small missions to Venus, such as those in NASA's Discovery Program, will not be up to the task of solving the outstanding problems, while at the same time making ambitious missions very hard to plan, because questions still remain about the environmental conditions they would have to work in. Before the tantalizing question of life above Venus can be answered, more basic spadework needs to be done, but neither NASA nor other space agencies are showing the necessary commitment.

That commitment could be crucial not just to understanding Venus but also Earth-sized planets around other stars. When scientists start detecting—and a decade or so later actually studying—such planets, they won't be little ones like Mars or moons like Europa. Researchers will be seeing planets the size of Earth and Venus. "What happens if we go out and we find primarily Venuses?" asks Crisp. Venus is both very much like Earth, in size and orbit and composition, and profoundly different. Without understanding these differences—including what they mean for the evolution of life on such planets—multibillion-dollar astrobiological efforts to make sense of Earth-like planets around other stars could be very frustrating.

Reprinted with permission from Oliver Morton, "Don't Ignore the Planet Next Door," SCIENCE 298:1706-1707. Copyright 2002 AAAS.

The Red Planet

No planet has captured the imagination of people on Earth as much as Mars has. Speculation has long raged over our nearest planetary neighbor, at once familiar and mysterious. New technologies are opening the way to a new understanding of Mars.

Among these new tools are the Thermal Emission Imaging System (THEMIS). This device is capable of using the heat given off by different types of materials to reveal information about the geologic composition of Mars. Thermal imaging has been used in the past to try to obtain data about Mars, but earlier systems were not capable of providing sufficiently clear data.

THEMIS has changed all of that. Contrary to the long-held popular image of Mars as a planet covered only in fine red dust, THEMIS has revealed that Mars contains areas with a diverse range of physical properties that geologists can use to map the surface of the

*planet and ultimately understand the nature of
its geologic evolution.—EF*

"The Surface of Mars: Not Just Dust and Rocks"
by Matthew P. Golombek
Science, June 27, 2003

The spectacular results from the Thermal Emission Imaging System (THEMIS) reported by Christensen et al. on page 2056 of this issue[1] resolve a long-simmering uncertainty about the value of thermal infrared measurements for understanding the bedrock geology of Mars.

Ever since the Viking orbiter returned thermal infrared measurements at roughly 1 [degree] (60 km) resolution,[2] scientists have argued about the utility of the resulting thermal inertia maps for identifying the bedrock geology, which is essential for deciphering the geologic history of Mars. Thermal inertia is a measure of the rate at which surface materials change temperature. It can be related to particle size and cohesion, such that large particles and cemented, fine-grained materials have higher thermal inertias than small particles or loosely bound, fine-grained materials.

The Viking infrared measurements showed broad areas with very low thermal inertia, indicative of surfaces dominated by very fine-grained, loosely bound dust. In other areas, up to a third of the surfaces are covered by individual rocks larger than 0.1 m in diameter, as seen at the Viking 1, Viking 2, and Mars Pathfinder landing sites.[3, 4] Because no outcrop or bare rock was evident at spatial scales of 60 km, thermal inertia and albedo have been used to map a "surface layer" on Mars related to eolian (wind) processes.

However, mapping eolian surface materials has little obvious relevance to the underlying bedrock geology, which has been typically inferred from surface morphology at scales of 1 km in Viking visible images. Thermal inertia data from Mars Global Surveyor Thermal Emission Spectrometer (TES) at a scale of 3 km/pixel showed an improved spatial relationship with inferred bedrock geology, but still did not offer fundamentally new insights into the underlying rock units.[5]

THEMIS data have forever changed the way geologists look at the surface of Mars. At a spatial scale of 100 m/pixel, thermal images of Mars show a large range in temperatures that allow the bedrock geology and the physical nature of the surfaces to be inferred directly. Certain areas have such high thermal inertia that they must be exposed bedrock. Other areas show differences in surface temperature that allow direct inference of particle sizes on the surface. These differences allow the definition of distinct contiguous geologic units that can be observed directly in the images.

Mars still exhibits areas that are covered by thick deposits of fine-grained, loosely bound dust. But other areas show a rich diversity of physical properties that will allow geologists to map geologic units based not only on their morphology in visible wavelengths, but also on their physical properties. Even fresh crater ejecta show up distinctively with rays of blocky or fine-grained materials; these variations in physical properties may be related to the age of the ejecta.

THEMIS has also collected visible images at a spatial scale of ~ 20 m/pixel. These images are also well suited to studying the bedrock geology. They show much more morphological detail than the global Viking orbital images at a scale of ~ 200 m/pixel. These images will help to determine the formation processes of geologic units on Mars. Furthermore, they will likely cover much more of Mars (hopefully global with an extended mission) than the higher resolution (~ 3 m/pixel) images from the Mars Orbiter Camera on Mars Global Surveyor.

By combining THEMIS thermal and visible images, planetary geologists will be able to map the entire surface with unprecedented insight into the geologic history and evolution of Mars. We can only guess at what startling new discoveries will be uncovered in the coming years as geologists remap Mars with this dramatic new data set.

References

1. P. R. Christensen et al., Science 300, 2056 (2003); published online 5 June 2003 (10.1126/science. 1080885).

2. H. H. Kieffer et al., J. Geophys. Res. 82, 4249 (1977).

3. P. R. Christensen, H. J. Moore, in Mars, H. H. Kieffer, B. M. Jakosky, C. W. Snyder, MI. S. Matthews, Eds. (Univ. of Arizona Press, Tucson, AZ, 1992), pp. 686-729.

4. M. P. Gotombek et al., Science 278, 1743 (1997).

5. M. T. Mellon et al., Icarus 148, 437 (2000).

6. F. D. Palluconi, H. H. Kieffer, Icarus, 45, 415 (1981).

Reprinted with permission from Matthew P. Golombek, "The Surface of Mars: Not Just Dust and Rocks," SCIENCE 300:2043-2044. Copyright 2003 AAAS.

One of the most central questions regarding Mars is, "Is there or was there water on Mars?" One of the reasons that this question is so pressing is that scientists have assumed that water would have been necessary if life as we know it were ever to have existed on the Red Planet. Although to date no traces of life have been found, evidence of water would mean that such an occurrence was not, in fact, impossible.

There has been plenty of evidence suggesting that the surface of Mars might have (at some point) been covered with water. Orbital photographs have revealed gorges, channels, and other features that may have been left by flowing water. The possibility remains, however, that such surface features were the result of volcanic activity or meteor impacts.

It wasn't until early 2004 that direct evidence of water on Mars was obtained. This occurred when Mars rovers crawling over the planet's surface started sending data on the composition of the rocks on Mars. The following article discusses the significance and implications of the latest discoveries about the composition of Mars.—EF

"The Blueberries of Mars: Was the Red Planet Once a Wet Planet? A Plucky Martian Rover Finally Delivers Some Hard Evidence"
by Jeffrey Kluger
Time, March 15, 2004

Giovanni Schiaparelli could have told you there had been water on Mars. It was Schiaparelli who peered through his telescope one evening in 1877 and discovered what he took to be the Red Planet's famous canals. As it turned out, the canals were an optical illusion, but as more powerful telescopes and, later, spacecraft zoomed in for closer looks, there was no shortage of clues suggesting that Mars was once awash in water. Photographs shot from orbit show vast plains that resemble ancient sea floors, steep gorges that would dwarf the Grand Canyon and sinuous surface scars that look an awful lot like dry riverbeds.

Given all that, why were NASA scientists so excited last week to announce that one of their Mars rovers, having crawled across the planet for five weeks, finally determined that Mars, at some point in its deep past, was indeed "drenched"—to use NASA's term—with liquid water?

Part of their excitement probably stems from sheer failure fatigue. NASA has had its share of setbacks in recent years—including a few disastrous missions to Mars. So it was with some relief that lead investigator Steve Squyres announced that the rover Opportunity had accomplished its primary mission. "The puzzle pieces have been falling into place," he told a crowded press conference, "and the last piece fell into place a few days ago."

But there was also, for the NASA team, the pleasure that comes from making a genuine contribution to space science. For despite all the signs pointing to Mars' watery past, until Opportunity poked its instruments into the Martian rocks, nobody was really sure how real that water was. At least some of the surface formations that look water carved could have been formed by volcanism and wind. Just two years ago, University of Colorado researchers published a persuasive paper suggesting that any water on Mars was carried in by crashing comets and then quickly evaporated.

The experiments that put that theory to rest—and nailed down the presence of water for good—were largely conducted on one 10-in.-high, 65-ft.-wide rock outcropping in the Meridiani Planum that mission scientists dubbed El Capitan. The surface of the formation is made up of fine layers—called parallel laminations—that are often laid down by minerals settling out of water. The rock is also randomly pitted with cavities called vugs that are created when salt crystals form in briny water and then fall out or dissolve away.

Chemical analyses of El Capitan, performed with two different spectrometers, support the visual evidence. They show that it is rich in sulfates known to form in the presence of water as well as a mineral called jarosite, which not only forms in water but also actually contains a bit of water trapped in its matrix.

The most intriguing evidence comes in the form of the BB-size spherules—or "blueberries," as NASA calls them—scattered throughout the rock. Spheres like these can be formed either by volcanism or by minerals accreting under water, but the way the blueberries are mixed randomly through the rock—not layered on top, as they would have been after a volcanic eruption—strongly suggests the latter.

None of these findings are dispositive, but their combined weight persuaded NASA scientists to summarize their findings in unusually explicit language. "We have concluded that the rocks here were soaked with liquid water," said Squyres flatly. "The ground would have been suitable for life."

Does that mean that there was—or still is—life on Mars? The fossil record on Earth suggests that given enough time and H_2O, life will eventually emerge, but there's nothing in the current findings to prove that this happened on Mars. Without more knowledge of such variables as temperature, atmosphere and the length of time Martian water existed, we can't simply assume that what happened on our planet would necessarily occur on another.

Opportunity and its twin robot Spirit are not equipped to search for life. Their mission is limited to looking for signs of water. But there's still a lot for them to do. Just knowing that rocks were wet doesn't tell you if the water was flowing or stationary, if it melted down from ice caps or seeped up through the ground. And if water was once there in such abundance, where did it go? Opportunity, which is very likely to exceed its planned 90-day mission, is already looking for those answers, toddling off to investigate other rocks farther and farther from its landing site. Spirit is conducting its own studies in Gusev Crater, on the opposite side of the planet.

The next step—the search for life—will have to wait until 2013 or so. That's when NASA has tentatively scheduled the first round trip to Mars—a mission that will pluck selected rocks off the Red Planet and bring them back home for closer study. Whether humans will ever follow those machines—President Bush's January announcement notwithstanding—is impossible to say.

Close, Closer, Closest

The rover Opportunity bounced down in the Meridiani Planum, just south of the Martian equator. The ancient plain looks a lot like a seabed, and mineral analysis, along with successive pictures by wide-angle cameras and a microscopic imager, suggests that's precisely what it was.

Getting to Work

The 65-ft.-wide outcropping that NASA has dubbed El Capitan was Opportunity's first target of close study. The rover's robotic arm carries a microscope, rock drill, spectrometers and other instruments.

Gathering Clues

The rock surface has fine layers that may have precipitated out of water, though wind or volcanoes could have been responsible. The so-called blueberries (color added by NASA) are scattered here and there.

Pay Dirt

The blueberries are actually the size of BB pellets and are probably minerals that accreted in water. If volcanoes had created them, they would be sprinkled on top, rather than mixed throughout.

© 2004 TIME Inc. reprinted by permission.

The images of dark streaks on Mars's surface have captivated scientists and laypeople for a long time. Pictures from the Mars Global Surveyor spacecraft's MOC (Mars Orbiter Camera) imager in 1999 revived that interest. These images also fueled the debate over whether these streaks were merely shadows in the dust or signs of water on the planet's surface. The streaks appear on crater and valley walls, widen on the downslope, and curve around dunes. Photos taken months apart show new streaks forming, but what are they?

Though many scientists attribute these streaks to dust avalanches, some of their features are inconsistent with that idea. This leads other scientists to wonder if they are the aftermath of liquid water that has seeped to the surface and receded again. The following article explores the idea that this may be the case. Whatever the nature of the streaks, the constant change they represent indicates that geophysical forces are still altering the face of Mars.—EF

"Does Mars Have Flowing Water?"
by Tahirih Motazedian
Astronomy, June 2004

Abstract: Dark streaks by the thousands run down the slopes of martian valleys and craters. They're dust avalanches, say most planetary scientists. But could any of these streaks be caused by groundwater seeps or springs?

Dark streaks on the slopes of martian hills, craters, and valleys have recently captivated scientists and space enthusiasts alike. These enigmatic features were first noted in Viking Orbiter photos decades ago, but the Mars Global Surveyor spacecraft's MOC imager photographed them with greater clarity starting in 1999. The MOC images have reinvigorated an old debate about whether Mars has water actively or intermittently flowing today on its surface.

The slope streaks are found on crater and valley walls. They widen downslope and weave around dunes, knobs, and crater rims. The streaks have no topographical relief, and they overlie existing surface features without perturbing them. MOC images taken months apart show new streaks are forming, making them some of the youngest surface features on Mars.

So what are these bizarre features? The answer most planetary scientists give is that the streaks are traces of dust avalanches. The answer is understandable; dust lies everywhere on Mars, settling continually from the air onto the ground, only to be picked up by the wind again and blown about. According to the conventional theory, some disturbance, high on a hillside where dust lies thick and the slope is steep, triggers a parcel of dust to begin sliding. Like snow, dust runs downhill, gathering more dust as it goes to make a dry avalanche. This removes a layer of surface dust, exposing the dark-colored martian basalt underneath.

But certain characteristics of dark slope-streaks are difficult to explain with the dust-avalanche model, leading some scientists to interpret these features as mineral stains left behind by liquid water flow. Similar features are sometimes observed in deserts on Earth, where groundwater seeps or springs leave behind trails of "rock varnish." Present conditions on Mars are such that pure water would immediately freeze and evaporate. But scientists are constructing theoretical models that show how liquid brines heavily laden with dissolved minerals can exist now on the surface of Mars.

Clues in the Dust

To understand the dark slope-streaks, it's worth exploring their characteristics, which may offer clues to their origin(s). Dark slope-streaks form in an equatorial band spanning from roughly 20 [degrees] south latitude to 40 [degrees] north. They concentrate in the volcanic regions of the Red Planet, being particularly dense in the vicinity of Olympus Mons. Towering 14 miles (22 kilometers) above a base that reaches 370 miles (600 km) across, it's the largest volcano in the solar system.

The dark streaks always appear on slopes, mostly crater and valley walls, but also on the flanks of small hills. The slopes are generally modest; one research group at the California Institute of Technology found that slope angles range from 16 [degrees] to 38 [degrees]. Dark slope-streaks are typically about one hundred feet (a few tens of meters) wide and hundreds of yards (meters) long.

These streaks differ from other dark martian surface features in a number of ways. They possess sharp boundaries, as opposed to the hazy margins of dust-devil tracks and wind streaks. The slope streaks also show a more uniform tone across their expanse than do other dark surface features. Unlike dust-devil tracks, which wind erratically in shape and direction, dark slope-streaks in a given area exhibit common trends in shape, distribution, and direction. Unlike wind streaks, which form diffuse patterns on plains, slope streaks always occur on slopes, strongly suggesting they are driven by gravity.

Dark streaks begin narrow at their upslope ends and widen downslope. They usually occur in clusters of parallel streaks, with most originating from a single rock layer. But while the top ends of the streaks generally line up, the bottom ends do not. Slope streaks often deflect around topographic obstacles, and many dark slope-streaks display strongly braided patterns. In certain locations, dark streaks overlie other surface features without disturbing them. Dark streaks never are seen to cause erosion. The slope streaks themselves have neither positive nor negative topographic relief; they appear simply as dark stains on the surface.

These features are among the youngest of all martian surface features—they are never cratered or overlain by other features such as sand dunes or by debris such as boulders or crater ejecta. Lighter-toned streaks also are seen, with the darker streaks overlying the lighter ones.

Not only are the dark streaks geologically young, they are forming currently, as shown by MOC photographs of the same area taken at different times. While no one can say exactly how long it takes for slope streaks to form, newly formed streaks have appeared in MOC images taken just months apart. California Institute of Technology researchers estimate roughly seventy new slope streaks form each martian day! Regardless of the process(es) creating these features, the martian surface is currently undergoing active change.

How to Make a Slope Streak

Planetary scientists know of a few ways to make dark slope-streaks. Gravity-driven slides such as dust avalanches could strip away light-colored surface dust to reveal darker materials beneath. Yet while this process probably does account for certain types of dark streaks, other streak characteristics don't seem to fit this theory.

For one thing, if these features were all caused by gravity-driven slumping of dry materials on slopes, we would expect to see them all over the planet, in any region with similar topography and materials. Slope streaks, however, form only in specific regions on Mars.

Lack of erosion and topographic relief are other sticking points with the dust-avalanche theory. No deposits of dust or debris are visible near the streaks, whereas if a path were being carved through dusty material on a slope, one would expect to see raised edges (levees) along the sides of the path. There would also be a pile-up of debris at the base of the slope.

Dark streaks overlie wind-generated (eolian) sand dunes and other surface features without erosion or disruption. This result is highly improbable if a mass of material was flowing over them. Slope streaks always originate with a sharp point-source and leave no apparent source scar. This is not typical of mass movements of material downslope, which tend to leave blunt, rounded head scarps. Some of the shapes of the dark streaks, particularly the braided patterns, suggest a highly fluid motion that's uncharacteristic of dry, gravity-driven mass movement.

Wind-driven processes do not appear to be a likely cause of slope streaks because of the streaks' sharply defined boundaries and uniform tone, and their consistent downslope attitude. The slope streaks bear distinctive shapes that are rarely (if ever) produced by wind streaks and dust-devil tracks. Moreover, the specific distribution of these streaks, running downslope in craters and valleys, is not consistent with formation by the broad, plains-sweeping action of the wind.

Going with the Flow

Liquid flow is the most promising process for explaining the majority of dark slope-streaks. This theory has been presented also by Justin Ferris and others working at the University of Arizona. Geothermal activity surrounding Olympus Mons may be causing subsurface ice to melt or otherwise driving liquid water to the surface from aquifers. It is possible that subsurface water dissolves minerals in the aquifer to form a brine, which leaches metals from silicates in the rocks.

The salts in the brine solution would lower the freezing temperature as well as the vapor pressure, allowing the mineral-rich water to flow at the martian surface. As the brine flows downhill, it leaves behind a trail of rock varnish formed by dark minerals that precipitate from solution. The lighter-toned streaks are likely older streaks that have become coated with light-colored surface dust over time.

The dark slope-streaks originate from distinct layers, or geologic horizons, below the martian surface, where the water/ice table meets crater and valley walls. The point-source origin of the dark streaks seems to indicate the piping of groundwater, as opposed to an aquifer-wide, broad flow. The braiding of the dark streaks indicates dynamic fluid motion. The fact that slope streaks neither build up topographic debris nor erode materials is consistent with small volumes of liquid trickling gently down a slope. The sharply defined ends of the dark streaks imply that the flows end where their liquid source is exhausted, having been consumed in coating surface dust and soaking back into the ground.

While the origin of dark slope-streaks isn't yet definitively known, it is very exciting to see the presence of currently active surface processes altering the face of Mars. The fact that there are daily changes invalidates the old idea that Mars is a dead planet. If these slope streaks in fact are being caused by the flow of liquid water, a flood of new scientific research and exploration will ensue, and fresh motivation and impetus will be instilled in the field of planetary space exploration.

Reproduced by permission. © 2004 *Astronomy* magazine, Kalmbach Publishing Co.

3 Ring Around the Planets

From October 1, 2000, to March 22, 2001, the Cassini *spacecraft made a close flyby of Jupiter to accelerate itself to reach Saturn. In the process of the flyby, Cassini's state-of-the-art camera setup took 26,000 pictures of Jupiter, its moons, and its rings. This data will provide valuable information that can ultimately be used to answer such questions as what is the source of the bands and eddies seen on the planet? Cassini's images of the polar region have revealed surprising new phenomena, such as the fading of Jupiter's bands and hundreds of interacting vortices.*

The data from Cassini has also confirmed some scientists' suspicions. Movies taken by Cassini's cameras show that Jupiter's moons, such as Metis and Adrastea, are the source of ring particles in Jupiter's faint and thin rings. These and other observations from Cassini's flyby are discussed in the following article.—EF

"Cassini Imaging at Jupiter"
by Larry Esposito
Science, March 7, 2003

On 30 December 2000, the Cassini spacecraft made its closest flyby to the planet Jupiter on its way to Saturn. For 6 months, Cassini's state-of-the-art cameras and other experiments watched the behavior of Jupiter, its magnetosphere, moons, and rings. The cameras provided an unsurpassed data set on atmospheric motions and other phenomena, reported by Porco et al. on page 1541 of this issue.[1] Cassini discovered surprising new phenomena and provided key information about Jupiter's meteorology, rings, and moons.

Cassini, a joint mission of NASA, ESA, and ASI (the Italian Space Agency), is the most ambitious planetary space mission ever launched. The spacecraft is nearly 7 m in length, carrying 12 experiments on its orbiter and six more on the European Huygens probe, which will land on Saturn's giant moon Titan. After launch on 15 October 1997, Cassini flew twice past the planet Venus, made a close approach to Earth, and then flew past Jupiter on the way to Saturn, where it will begin orbiting on 1 July 2004. The Huygens probe will descend through Titan's atmosphere, directly sampling its composition before landing on 14 January 2005. On Titan's cold surface, the probe will hopefully survive for more than 30 min, sending pictures and analysis of the surface back to Earth, using the orbiter as a radio relay link.

In December 2000 and January 2001, both the Cassini spacecraft and the NASA Galileo orbiter were in the close vicinity of Jupiter, providing the first-ever conjunction of two spacecraft at an outer planet.

Nearly simultaneous measurements were also made by the Hubble Space Telescope and the Chandra X-ray Observatory from Earth orbit. Because Galileo's high-gain antenna failed to open, the spacecraft has very limited communication to Earth and cannot provide the larger picture of Jupiter meteorology. Cassini scientists and engineers took this opportunity to take simultaneous measurements with the Galileo spacecraft, to provide a long continuous look at the Jupiter system, and to test their experiments in preparation for the 4-year tour of the Saturn system. The first Cassini imaging results are presented by Porco et al. in this issue.[1] Cassini measurements of the Jupiter radiation environment, which complement the imaging results reported here, have been published previously.[2]

During the Jupiter flyby, the Cassini camera system collected 26,000 images between 1 October 2000 and 22 March 2001. The main purpose of the flyby was to accelerate the spacecraft on to Saturn. At the closest approach of 9.72 million km (136 times Jupiter's radius), the images have a resolution of 58 km, not as good as the best images sent back by Voyager (during its 1979 flyby) and Galileo. But Cassini spectacularly succeeded in providing 6 months of global, continuous viewing of Jupiter's atmosphere.

It is too soon to say whether these data can answer the question of the ultimate source of the bands and eddies on Jupiter. Do these arise from small convective storms gradually aggregating into the large, organized motion? Do the larger storms thus "feed" on this energy source to sustain their long existence? The "Great Red Spot" is a centuries-old hurricane that could hold several Earths. The Cassini images show it gobbling up several smaller storms,[1] supporting this scenario.

Cassini's observations of Jupiter's polar region have been assembled into a movie that shows surprising new phenomena. Toward the poles, Jupiter's banded appearance fades, and hundreds of interacting vortices are seen. Small-scale features north of 60 [degrees] latitude grow and disappear in a period of weeks. A large dark oval—as big as the Great Red Spot—grew, developed a bright core, began to circulate clockwise, and finally elongated and thinned, gradually disappearing. This storm may have been triggered by an event in Jupiter's magnetosphere: Its location coincides with the region where particles from Jupiter's radiation belts enter the atmosphere,[3] causing bright aurorae (like the northern lights on Earth). Cassini is now planning comparable observations of Saturn's polar regions to seek similar phenomena there.

The Cassini cameras observed aurorae on the back side of Jupiter while simultaneous measurements were made by Hubble from Earth orbit. These data confirm that the auroral region is larger on the night side, as expected from variation in the pressure of the solar wind. The moons Io and Europa were photographed when eclipsed from the Sun by Jupiter, showing visible glows from electrons that strike their thin atmospheres. These observations will be fruitfully compared with those from Hubble to better characterize this atmospheric phenomenon.[4]

Movies of Jupiter's very faint and thin rings confirm that small moons like Metis and Adrastea are the immediate source of the ring particles. The meteoritic bombardment of these objects knocks off dust particles that then form the visible ring around Jupiter. Porco et al. make good use of the particular angles at which Cassini observed to argue that the ring particles are not spherical, as was previously assumed.

The Cassini Jupiter flyby was a great success, helping to prepare for the Cassini Saturn mission and providing key data sets (including images and movies) about the meteorology of Jupiter, its moons, magnetosphere, and ring system. Saturn has only been visited briefly by Pioneer (1979) and the two Voyager spacecrafts (1980, 1981). The planned 4-year orbital mission will allow long-term studies and follow-up observations of new discoveries. The Jupiter results provide some hints of the spectacular new findings that await Cassini when it reaches Saturn.

References
1. C. C. Porco et al., Science 299, 1541 (2003).
2. T. W. Hill, Nature 415, 965 (2002).
3. J. T. Clarke et al., Nature 415, 997 (2002).
4. M. A. McGrath et al., Bull. Am. Astron. Soc., DPS meeting abstract 34.09 (2000).

Reprinted with permission from Larry Esposito, "Cassini Imaging at Jupiter," SCIENCE 299:1529-1530. Copyright 2003 AAAS.

Observing a planet directly through an orbiting spacecraft or surface probes is not the only way to understand the forces that formed it. Two teams of scientists are attempting experiments designed to help us understand the nature of Jupiter's core. Jupiter is composed mainly of hydrogen, and the intense pressures at the planet's core should cause this hydrogen to act like liquid metal. However, no one has been able to tell what such a substance would be like because it is impossible to reproduce that kind of compression of hydrogen in a lab.

Recently, however, two research teams have released data that sheds light on what might be happening in Jupiter's core. A team at Lawrence Livermore National Laboratory in California and a separate group at Sandia National Laboratories in Albuquerque, New Mexico, have squashed a substance called deuterium with millions of atmospheres of pressure. Deuterium is chemically the same as hydrogen, but it is denser. This makes it easier to use for this purpose.

Although both groups succeeded in compressing the deuterium, achieving a change into a metallic state, the two teams disagree about what happens in Jupiter's core. The following article explains how the scientists achieved their results, the significance of their

*achievement, and what the two teams think
happens at the core.—EF*

"By Jove! If You Go Down to the Planet's Core, You're Sure of a Big Surprise"
by Eugenie Samuel
New Scientist, April 27, 2002

Two teams are racing to reach the core of Jupiter. Not by actually boring into the giant planet, but by squeezing hydrogen to incredibly high pressures to simulate what it's like there. The results could tell us the maximum possible size of a planet like Jupiter—if only the two teams could agree on what they mean.

Jupiter is made mainly of hydrogen, and in the centre of the planet it is crushed by pressures millions of times the air pressure on Earth. Under these conditions, physicists reckon hydrogen should behave like a liquid metal. But no one has been able to investigate what this material will be like because researchers had only managed to compress hydrogen up to a few hundred thousand atmospheres until recently.

Now a team at the Lawrence Livermore National Laboratory in California, and a rival group at Sandia National Laboratories in Albuquerque, New Mexico, have squashed deuterium to millions of atmospheres. Deuterium is chemically identical to hydrogen but denser, making it easier to generate high-pressure shock waves in. At Sandia, Marcus Knudsen's team used an intense magnetic field to accelerate metal plates and smash them into a deuterium target at 20 kilometres per second. At Livermore, Robert Cauble and his colleagues compressed their deuterium using a shock wave generated by the super-powerful Nova laser.

Both groups reported their results this week at the American Physical Society meeting in Albuquerque. They found that the deuterium began to turn shiny, a sign it was becoming metallic. To their surprise they found that this happened only gradually, suggesting that there is no hard boundary to Jupiter's metallic core. Many theorists had predicted a sudden phase change into the metallic form.

But the two teams disagree about what happens within the core. Researchers at Livermore say that at the pressures they reached, the metallic deuterium's density was twice that claimed by the Sandia team. Cauble says this leads to a 15 per cent disagreement about how large and dense Jupiter's metallic core is.

It would also affect how big a planet can possibly be. The denser hydrogen becomes when compressed, the easier it is for nuclear fusion to start, turning a planet into a star.

Deciding who is right may have to wait for future space missions, which could reveal the size of Jupiter's metallic core via precise measurements of its gravitational field.

It's possible that two groups are measuring slightly different things. The Sandia method compresses deuterium for about five times as long as the Livermore team. This should mean their measurements more closely reflect what is happening in Jupiter's core, where the gas is in equilibrium.

But Cauble thinks the Livermore results could still be relevant, because planetary cores aren't always in equilibrium. In 1994, Comet Shoemaker-Levy crashed into Jupiter, causing shock waves that reverberated around the whole planet. They could have disturbed the core, he thinks, perhaps briefly increasing its size.

Reprinted with permission from *New Scientist*.

Unlike the solid, rocky, terrestrial planets—Mercury, Earth, Mars, and Venus—Jupiter and Saturn are giant gas planets. Although rocky planets like Earth may be discovered to be orbiting other stars in the universe, gas giants are likely to be rare. How Jupiter and Saturn formed is a puzzling question.

The atmospheres of both planets are composed of helium and hydrogen. This would have to have been captured gravitationally from the young Sun when they were formed, but the area around Sun-like stars doesn't contain much gas. If the Sun had more gas around it in its early days, Jupiter and Saturn must have formed quickly and grabbed it fast.

In an attempt to find out how these gas giants might have formed, Ben M. Zuckerman of the University of California, Los Angeles, Thierry Forveille of Grenoble Observatory in France, and Joel H. Kastner of the Massachusetts Institute of Technology have studied twenty Sun-like stars. Their findings seem to indicate that Saturn and Jupiter are unusual indeed.—EF

"The Importance of Being Jupiter"
Science News, **February 18, 1995**

If stars other than the sun have planets, those orbiting bodies probably don't match Jupiter and Saturn in size and composition. In fact, even if rocky, terrestrial planets akin to Mars or Venus prove abundant, Jupiterlike gas giants may well be rarities. A new report lends support to that intriguing notion.

Scientists have long argued that the planets in our solar system formed from a disk of gas and dust that surrounded the nascent sun. Because Jupiter and Saturn have massive atmospheres of helium and hydrogen, they must have captured these gases gravitationally from the solar disk.

That may pose a problem. The vicinity of ordinary, sunlike stars has little gas, suggesting that hydrogen and helium aren't easily retained in orbit as these stars mature. For example, the solar system now contains only a few percent of the hydrogen and helium needed to make Jupiter and Saturn. Thus, the planets must have formed rapidly (SN: 3/27/93, p.198).

It's possible that the sun's environs once contained much more hydrogen and helium. But according to George W. Wetherill of the Carnegie Institution of Washington (D.C.), a middle-aged, stable star like the sun of today couldn't have blown away such large quantities of gas recently. However, the sun might have done so during its turbulent first few million years. If so, the gas giants Jupiter and Saturn must have grabbed their helium and hydrogen early.

Astronomers can't turn back the clock to find out how much hydrogen the infant solar system contained. But by examining the amount of this gas around young, sunlike stars, they can attempt to determine whether these stars possess the raw materials needed to make Jupiters and Saturns.

In their study, Ben M. Zuckerman of the University of California, Los Angeles, Thierry Forveille of Grenoble Observatory in France, and Joel H. Kastner of the Massachusetts Institute of Technology examined 20 nearby, sunlike stars with estimated ages of between 1 and 10 million years—presumably young enough that they would not yet have blown hydrogen and helium out of their vicinity. Using the 30-meter IRAM radio telescope in Pico Veleta, Spain, the group inferred the density of molecular hydrogen. Because this molecule doesn't emit radio waves, the team measured the abundance of carbon monoxide, which exists around sunlike stars in a specific ratio to hydrogen.

The team reports in the Feb. 9 Nature that even stars just a few million years old typically have much less molecular hydrogen than the mass of Jupiter in their environs. "Thus, if gas-giant planets are common in the galaxy, they must form even more quickly than present models suggest," the researchers conclude; more likely, the planets have only a small chance of forming.

In a commentary accompanying the report, Wetherill speculates that the existence of Jupiter and Saturn in our own planetary system could be a statistical fluke. He adds, however, that these planets serve to protect Earth, deflecting or ejecting comets that might otherwise bombard our planet. Without Jupiter and Saturn, Earth might not contain life to ponder the existence of these giants.

SCIENCE NEWS by Staff. Copyright by SCI SERVICE INC. Reproduced with permission of SCI SERVICE INC in the textbook format via Copyright Clearance Center.

Celestial mechanics are the rules that govern how planets and other bodies move in relation to each other. Since Newton first described his physical laws, scientists have used them to explain and predict a wide range of phenomena in the solar system. It has all worked like clockwork—until recently, when two moons of Saturn, Prometheus and Pandora, were found to be exhibiting odd behavior in their orbits. This behavior was contrary to what would be expected from the rules of celestial mechanics. While data from the Hubble Space Telescope has revealed more information, the mystery regarding what could be causing the moons' odd orbital behavior has only become greater. The following article describes the mysteries of these moons' behavior, reviews the data provided by sources such as the Hubble telescope,

*and explores some possible reasons for such
odd behavior.—EF*

"Moon Behaving Badly: Why Won't Two of Saturn's Satellites Obey the Rules?"
by Govert Schilling
New Scientist, April 6, 2002

Celestial mechanics is the grand old lady of science—reliable, precise, unfaltering. Ever since Newton drafted his laws of gravity and mechanics, scientists have used them to predict conjunctions and eclipses, to discover new planets on the basis of tiny gravitational disturbances, and to send spacecraft to the ends of the Solar System. It's all so predictable that we know where the planets and their moons will be thousands of years from now.

But two tiny satellites of Saturn seem intent on being the naughty children in the class. Between 1981 and 1995, these two moons changed speed, apparently defying the laws of gravity. Last summer they misbehaved again, and no one knows why. Could this mean there's something about celestial mechanics that we're missing?

The two satellites were discovered on photographs snapped by NASA's Voyager 1 spacecraft when it flew past Saturn more than 20 years ago. Called Prometheus and Pandora, they orbit in the outer suburbs of Saturn's spectacular ring system, speeding around the planet in only 15 hours.

That brief fly-by didn't give astronomers enough information to establish the moons' orbits, but they didn't have long to wait before Voyager 2 took another set of photos in August 1981. From the movement of Prometheus and Pandora in the nine months between the two observations, astronomers calculated their orbits. From this, they were able to predict the moons' positions for any time in the future. Or so they assumed.

Nothing happened for almost 14 years. No new observations, no checks on the predictions. After all, why would anyone doubt the inevitable progress of celestial mechanics? Then, in the spring of 1995, a team led by Amanda Bosh of Lowell Observatory in Flagstaff, Arizona, took a look at Saturn and its tiny moons with the Hubble Space Telescope during a brief period in which the rings were seen almost edge-on. Pandora turned up exactly where it was supposed to be, but Prometheus was lagging 19 [degrees] behind its predicted position. The satellite had apparently slowed down since the early 1980s, implying that it had drifted slightly away from the planet.

The astronomers were shocked. Prometheus and Pandora are quite small as moons go, but even so each is comparable in size to Northern Ireland or Connecticut, and must weigh many trillions of tonnes. So what could have pushed one of them tens of thousands of kilometres out of place?

One possibility is that Prometheus had been hit by a small asteroid or comet, but that's extremely unlikely. Realistically, the only force strong enough to have had such an effect is gravity. But the gravity of what? Theorists thought they had taken everything into account, but now they had to dream up some new explanations for the lag in Prometheus's motion. One was that there is some undiscovered moon in the same orbit as Prometheus, influencing its orbit. But to have the observed effect, this extra satellite would have to be fairly big, so the Voyagers should have seen it.

A more promising explanation came from Carl Murray of Queen Mary University of London: he suggested that Prometheus was interacting with one of Saturn's rings. The moon orbits just inside the F-ring, a thin stream of debris that circles Saturn a little way outside the main ring system. Although Prometheus is usually a few hundred kilometres away from the ring, too far for gravity to have much effect, every 19 years or so there is a period when its orbit takes the moonlet almost into the ring during each revolution. Might there be enough mass in the F-ring to slightly change Prometheus's orbit?

The only way to test this idea was to keep a close eye on the misbehaving moon, and Richard French of Wellesley College, Massachusetts, again used the Hubble telescope to keep watch. In 1997 graduate student Colleen McGhee, based at Cornell University in Ithaca, New York, analysed the Hubble observations in the hope of finally tying Prometheus down. But instead of solving the mystery she discovered another one: Pandora was misbehaving too. Every 633 days, it speeded up, drifting away from its average position by almost a degree, before slowing down again and drifting back.

Although this was a surprise, it wasn't hard to come up with an explanation. Pandora's orbital period of 15 hours is almost exactly two-thirds that of Mimas, a much larger moon of Saturn. So the two moons are nearly in an "orbital resonance": after three orbits of

Pandora, Mimas has gone around Saturn twice, and they're back in roughly the same relative position. This means that slight gravitational tugs between the two moons won't cancel each other out over time, as they would normally. Instead they are likely to add up to produce a relatively large effect—Pandora's oscillation.

But this raised another problem. When the oscillation caused by resonance with Mimas was included in the calculations, it turned out that Pandora shouldn't have been where it was seen in 1995 after all: it was about as far ahead of where it belonged as Prometheus was lagging behind. "It was a complete coincidence that Pandora looked OK," says Luke Dones, a planetary scientist at the Southwest Research Institute in Boulder, Colorado.

Suddenly, here were two satellites thumbing their noses at celestial mechanics. Both theories that had been suggested to explain the behaviour of Prometheus became obsolete. If a co-orbital satellite was the culprit in Prometheus's case, astronomers would have to assume that another co-orbital of almost the same size was having the same effect on Pandora. If interactions with the F-ring were to blame, it was a mystery why Pandora would show a similar effect, since it never gets closer to the F-ring than 1000 kilometres or so.

If news had got out, headlines might have read "Newton proved wrong." But the awkward results were only discussed at conferences, and never published. French and his colleagues planned to publish them last September—but then new Hubble results revealed another mystifying twist.

Prometheus and Pandora had apparently changed gear again, right under the astronomers' noses. For some reason, Prometheus's average distance to Saturn increased by a few hundred metres, while Pandora's orbit shrank by about the same amount. No one has the faintest idea why. "This is real terra incognita," says French.

The only glimmer of an explanation is coming from computer simulations at Boulder by Dones and Hal Levison. In a model of Pandora-like orbits, they occasionally see sudden jumps in orbital radius. This, they think, is because Pandora has orbital resonances with moons besides Mimas. These would add up to make Pandora's motion chaotic. Hence its odd behaviour.

But Prometheus doesn't have any orbital resonances. Murray thinks that the F-ring could still play a role, especially if it proves to be fringed by stray objects much larger than the rocks that make up the narrow visible ring.

So for now, the mystery remains. If it isn't solved within the next two years, NASA's Cassini spacecraft should do the job. Due to arrive in orbit around Saturn in mid-2004, Cassini will repeatedly survey the whole F-ring region. As well as determining the positions of Prometheus and Pandora much more precisely, Cassini could find minimoons as small as a few kilometres across, perhaps including Murray's stray objects.

Prometheus and Pandora's behaviour could have a significance far beyond Saturn. The giant planet's system of rings and small satellites is a miniature version of the dusty discs around stars in which planets are believed to form. It's still speculation, but understanding the resonances that control Saturn's moons could provide clues about the processes that shape solar systems—and perhaps created our planet.

Reprinted with permission from *New Scientist.*

On December 7, 1995, the Galileo space probe passed by Jupiter, sending data on the giant planet back to scientists on Earth. What this data showed shattered many of the scientists' assumptions about the nature of Jupiter. For example, much to their surprise, Jupiter's atmosphere contains neither clouds nor water, and lightning is rare. In contrast to materials such as oxygen, helium, carbon, and neon, which they expected to find on Jupiter, they found that the planet's composition is much more like that of the Sun. In addition, the probe revealed that Jupiter is surrounded by a belt of radiation. These discoveries have led scientists to reconsider how Jupiter and the other gas giants formed. The following article provides a detailed look at what Galileo has revealed about the composition of Jupiter. It also discusses the models that scientists have developed to explain the solar system.—EF

"Into the Maelstrom"
by Robert Burnham
Astronomy, April 1996

Abstract: Galileo made observations on Jupiter on Dec. 7, 1995, that shattered previous notions about the planet. Jupiter lacks the three layers of clouds previously perceived, and no water was detected in the thin clouds present. Jupiter's composition is closer to the Sun's than previously thought.

The spacecraft fell out of the late afternoon sky toward the streaming cloud deck. After riding a trail of ionized gas thousands of kilometers long, the craft opened its parachute, turned on its instruments, and began a controlled fall into the Jovian maelstrom. An hour later, the Galileo probe's mission was over—but the vital information about the giant planet was safely on board the Galileo orbiter for transmittal to Earth.

The Jupiter that the probe sampled on December 7, 1995, differed significantly from scientists' expectations. First, Jupiter's composition tested more like the Sun than anyone had figured. Next, not only did the entry site lack the expected three layers of cloud, but its thin clouds contained no water, which the Voyager measurements and the Shoemaker-Levy 9 impacts indicated was there. Also, lightning was relatively rare and seems to have generated no complex organic molecules. The atmosphere itself was both denser and windier than scientists had guessed, and the winds did not slacken as the probe descended. Finally, the probe found an unsuspected radiation belt extending from Jupiter's filmy dust ring down almost to its cloudtops.

"There's always a sense of humility when the data come in," sighs Galileo chief project scientist Torrance Johnson, of the Jet Propulsion Laboratory. "The results don't fit our models very well . . . the shoe pinches!"

The probe had been on course for Jupiter since parting from the orbiter six months before. Its target: a spot in the Jovian clouds on the southern edge of the North Equatorial Belt, at 6.6 [degrees] north latitude and 4.4 [degrees] west longitude. While every location on Jupiter is a swirling mosaic of gas, scientists chose this site because they hoped it would be as representative of the "normal" Jupiter as possible.

Jupiter's menu of surprises opened before the probe had tasted even the first wisp of Jovian air. In the hours before entry, the probe's instruments detected a new, energetic radiation belt of charged particles. "No spacecraft had ever gone inside the dust ring before," notes Richard Young of NASA's Ames Research Center, the probe's chief scientist. The new belt extends from the dust ring (at 1.8 Jupiter radii) down toward the cloudtops and is at least ten times stronger than Earth's radiation belts.

"We don't know where these high-energy particles come from," says Harald Fischer of the University of Kiel, Germany, a scientist working on the energetic particle detector. The particles reach maximum strength, he notes, about 50,000 kilometers above the cloudtops. It will take more study, and data from the orbiter, to unravel the puzzle of where the particles in the new belt originate.

When the probe finally began its entry, the first touch of the Jovian atmosphere was lost, scientists say, because for unknown reasons the data collection began 53 seconds late. But despite this, the probe recorded another surprise: a relative lack of clouds.

At an altitude where the pressure was about a third of a bar (1 bar = Earth's surface pressure), the probe detected a layer of what may have been thin ammonia cirrus. Its evanescent quality was unexpected. Based on models using Voyager and Shoemaker-Levy data, scientists had anticipated a thicker and denser layer here. And this pattern continued. Below the cirrus the probe found a cloud of ammonium hydrosulfide that was about as thick as light fog or mist on Earth, hardly the big piles of cumulus clouds that models had predicted. Lower still, where scientists looked to find water clouds, the probe detected nothing. Besides being almost cloud-free, the atmosphere was unexpectedly warm and completely dry, with no trace of water vapor or ice.

The lack of water was surprising, but perhaps the biggest jolt involved the composition of Jupiter's atmosphere. It contains a riddle that will worry theorists until they fully understand it.

Scientists had expected to find Jupiter enriched (relative to the Sun's composition) in water, oxygen, carbon, helium, neon, and other materials. What they got, however, was a Jupiter much more Sun-like in its makeup. And this has implications for ideas on how nature makes a Jupiter and other gas-giant planets.

Two contrasting models have sought to explain the origin of Jupiter. One says Jupiter formed from the same materials as the Sun, but stopped growing before it could become a second star. The other model says that Jupiter formed the way Earth did—out of rocky planetesimals—but in a colder part of the solar system. Being cold let Jupiter also accrete hordes of icy planetesimals, comets and asteroids rich in carbon compounds. If the first model was right, Jupiter would be solar in composition. If the second was right, Jupiter would have extra amounts of water, carbon, and so on.

What the probe found was a Sun-like Jupiter. This poses a big problem for theorists. Why? Because a lot of them had convinced themselves that Jupiter followed the second path to formation. Galileo's findings are awkward for theorists, to say the least.

The composition measurements also say something else is missing: complex organic molecules. This, project scientists think, is due to the relative scarcity of Jovian lightning, which provides energy to synthesize such molecules.

"We built a sophisticated transistor radio in hopes of detecting [lightning], like you can pick up static on your car radio," says probe investigator Lou Lanzerotti of Bell Laboratories. "But we didn't know what to expect." Voyager had imaged flashes of lightning, and the probe's instrument was designed to pick up any bolts within about 10,000 km of the craft. The probe detected some 50,000 individual lightning bolts, but this is 3 to 10 times less than the rate found on Earth.

As the probe plummeted—it fell at about 100 miles an hour—its ride was anything but smooth. Unlike Earth's winds, driven by solar heating, Jupiter's weather comes from within. "Jupiter's winds appear to originate in the heat from the deep interior," says Young. He compared the ride to that of an airplane flying through a major storm. "You certainly wouldn't have wanted to be inside!"

Scientists expected that the winds would diminish as the probe sank deeper. Instead, by the time the probe fell silent, the winds had strengthened from 360 km/hour at the cloudtops to 540 km/hr at last measurement. By this point, 150 km below the altitude when the probe began its data-taking, it had reached a depth where the pressure was 22 bars and the outside temperature was 300 [degrees] F. Bouncing on its shroud lines and buffetted by turbulent winds, the probe lost contact with the orbiter and its mission ended, 57 minutes after it began.

What happened then? No one knows how the probe met its end. But its fate can be guessed by the materials it was made from. The Dacron parachute probably melted about an hour after the last signals were sent. With the parachute gone, the probe fell quickly into the hot dark depths. Roughly 40 minutes later, at a temperature of 1,200 [degrees] F and a pressure of 260 bars, the aluminum in the probe softened and turned liquid. Blobs of molten aluminum streamed off the plummeting probe like hot wax off a lit candle. Vaporizing, they became part of Jupiter.

Many more parts of the probe—pieces of planet Earth in an utterly alien environment—suffered the same fate. The last major item to go was the titanium hull. Titanium doesn't melt until 3,100 [degrees] F, which comes at a depth of 2,000 bars. The end was quick. As the hull became molten, it broke into droplets. Then these too flashed into gas and vanished into Jupiter's roiling atmosphere.

The probe's mission is over. But for the orbiter, it's just beginning. Flight controllers spent February playing back the tape recorder, double and triple-checking that all the data have been sent correctly back to Earth.

In March, mission controllers fire the craft's engine to increase the distance at which the orbiter comes closest to Jupiter. (This is necessary because a second pass through the intense radiation belts near Io would probably destroy the spacecraft's electronics.) In April, the spacecraft gets a rest from housekeeping chores and can do some science. But later in April, new flight control software has to be loaded into the orbiter and checked out. That will take until about the middle of May.

Then the craft will be on course and ready for its first close-up satellite encounter, with Ganymede, on June 27, 1996.

Reproduced by permission. © 2004 *Astronomy* magazine, Kalmbach Publishing Co.

In 1659, Christiaan Huygens, a Dutch astronomer, first identified that Saturn was surrounded by "a thin, flat ring, nowhere touching." Later in the seventeenth century, this description was expanded by Jean-Dominique Cassini, a

Franco-Italian astronomer. At this point, the division between the inner and outer rings was dubbed the Cassini division. It is now known that Saturn is not unique but is instead one of at least four ringed planets. However, all rings are not alike. Saturn and Uranus have rings made of ice particles. Jupiter's rings appear to be composed of rock. Meanwhile, no one is certain as to what Neptune's rings are composed of. Not long after it was first discovered that Saturn possessed rings, scientists began asking what they were made of. The following article explores the nature of planetary rings.—EF

"Rings Around the Planets"
by Richard Panek
Natural History, October 2000

Saturn's most prominent feature is no longer a singular phenomenon. Saturn is the ringed planet, right? Wrong. A little over twenty years ago, it was demoted to a far less privileged position in the solar system: a ringed planet. To be precise, it is merely one of four— or possibly more—such celestial objects.

Saturn's seemingly distinctive look has been an object of astronomical fascination since July 1610, when Galileo first observed the planet's "triple-bodied" appearance through a telescope and tried (although unsuccessfully) to explain it (see "The Sharp-Eyed Lynx Outfoxed by Nature," Natural History, May 1998). It wasn't until 1659 that the Dutch astronomer Christiaan Huygens, working with better equipment and more favorable viewing conditions, finally announced a solution to the puzzle: "a thin, flat ring, nowhere touching."

Thin, flat rings, actually, as French-Italian astronomer Jean-Dominique Cassini determined in 1675. (Thereafter, the space between the inner and outer rings was called the Cassini Division.) Having figured out that Saturn actually had rings, astronomers next asked themselves: Why rings, of all things? Specifically, are the rings of Saturn solid, or are they . . . something else?

Definitely something else, said French theoretician Pierre-Simon Laplace, who in 1785 proved mathematically that the rotation rates of solid rings would violate Kepler's third law of planetary motion. As to what that something else might be, Laplace had a suggestion: not two rings but millions of rings, all rotating at varying rates. In 1856 the British astronomer James Clerk Maxwell refined that hypothesis, arriving at an interpretation more in keeping with the satellite pattern elsewhere evident in the solar system: not millions of rings but millions of moonlets. Indeed, American astronomer James E. Keeler validated this interpretation in 1895 through spectroscopic observation.

There the matter of planetary rings more or less rested until March 10, 1977. On that day, two groups of astronomers observed the disappearance (occultation) of a ninth-magnitude star behind Uranus. One group of astronomers, aboard an airborne observatory, noticed several spikes on the data plot just before the star vanished from view, indicating some sort of irregularity in the immediate vicinity of the planet. On a hunch, the researchers radioed the ground-based team and urged them to continue gathering data when the star reemerged from behind Uranus. Sure enough, the second group of astronomers found an identical set of spikes at the same distance from the planet. The only possible explanation was rings.

Suddenly Saturn's centuries-old reign as the ringed planet was over. Then, visits of the Voyager 1 spacecraft to Jupiter in 1979 and of Voyager 2 to Neptune in 1989 revealed that they too had ring systems. Some astronomers have even hypothesized the presence of very thin rings around Mars as well (they're looking). Apparently rings are a common feature among planets—a realization that has only complicated astronomers' efforts to study what rings are, where they came from, and how they work.

The rings of Saturn and Uranus appear to consist primarily of ice particles, ranging in size from mote to iceberg, while Jupiter's seem to be rock. Neptune's rings, however, remain a mystery. The particles that comprise the rings of these four planets might be relics from the formation of the solar system or remnants of moons that broke apart after venturing too close to the planet, or maybe of moons that suffered from violent collisions. Whatever their source, these particles have settled over the eons into a central plane, apparently stabilized by the host planet's gravitational field.

Still, mathematicians have shown that gravity alone can't explain why millions of particles would maintain a ring shape over time. One further possible explanation has met with great success: bodies called "shepherding moons" may gravitationally corral the particles. Predicted in 1979, they've since been photographed around Saturn and Uranus. But even after more extensive and precise surveys of these shepherds have been conducted, the mechanics of rings will probably remain, as one planetary specialist recently told a meeting of the American Astronomical Society, "hideously complicated."

Despite the discoveries of the past two decades, Saturn does retain its distinction as the only planet whose rings are visible through telescopes available to the backyard astronomer. By the end of October, the planet will be nearer to Earth than at any time since February 1977. Coincidentally, the planet's tilt will leave the rings more "open" to view than they have been in nine years. Check the eastern sky about two hours after nightfall. One look through even a modest telescope and you'll see for yourself that even though this ringed planet may no longer be singular, it remains no less spectacular.

Reprinted from *Natural History* October 2000; copyright © *Natural History* Magazine, Inc. 2000.

4 Giants in the Sky

The motion of the planets that seem to wander across the sky has fascinated people since earliest times. The first eight planets in the solar system can be divided into two groups according to their basic composition. One group consists of the so-called Jovian planets—Jupiter, Saturn, Neptune, and Uranus—and the other group is made up of Earth and its terrestrial neighbors—Mercury, Venus, and Mars. (Pluto is different from either of these two groups.)

Although it shares many characteristics in common with Jupiter, Saturn, and Neptune, Uranus also exhibits some puzzling features in its composition and orbit. For example, unlike the other Jovian planets, which have cores that generate a great deal of heat, Uranus's core gives off very little heat; in this way it's more like Earth. For another example, Uranus lies on its side as it orbits the Sun, unlike all the other planets, which orbit upright. The following article provides both a historical overview of the discovery of the planets in our solar system and an *illuminating look at what recent discoveries have revealed about the secrets of Uranus.—EF*

"The First New Planet"
by Carl Sagan
Astronomy, **March 1995**

Abstract: Observers of the solar system had long thought that it contained seven planets, until a musician and amateur astronomer named William Herschel discovered Uranus in 1781. Later, after astrophysicists pieced together facts about Uranus's surface and atmosphere, they discovered Uranus's rings.

Before we invented civilization, our ancestors lived mainly in the open, out under the sky. Before artificial lights, atmospheric pollution, and modern forms of nocturnal entertainment, people watched the stars. Star watching had practical calendrical reasons, but there was more to it than that. Even today, the most jaded city dweller can be unexpectedly moved by a clear night studded with thousands of stars. When it happens to me after all these years as a professional astronomer, it still takes my breath away.

I lie back in an open field and the sky surrounds me. I'm overpowered by its scale. It is so vast and so far away that my own insignificance becomes palpable. I'm a part of it—tiny to be sure, but everything is tiny compared to that overwhelming immensity. And when I concentrate on the stars, the planets, and their motions, I have an irresistible sense of clockwork—elegant precision working on a scale that, however lofty our aspirations, dwarfs and humbles us.

Most of the great inventions in human history—from stone tools and the domestication of fire to written language—were made by unknown benefactors. Our institutional memory of long-gone events is feeble. We do not know the name of that ancestor who first noticed that planets were different from stars. She or he lived tens, perhaps hundreds of thousands of years ago. But eventually, people all over the world understood that five, and no more, of the bright points of light that grace the night sky break lockstep with the others over a period of months, moving strangely.

Sharing the odd apparent motion of these planets were the Sun and Moon, making seven wandering bodies in all. These seven were important to the ancients, so they named the wanderers after gods—not any old gods, but the chief gods, the ones that tell other gods (and mortals) what to do. One of the planets, bright and slow moving, was named by the Babylonians after Marduk, by the Norse after Odin, and by the Romans after Jupiter, in each case after the king of the gods. The faint, fast-moving one that was never far from the Sun the Romans named Mercury, after the messenger of the gods. The most brilliant of them they named Venus, after the goddess of love and beauty; blood red Mars, after the god of war; and the most sluggish of the bunch Saturn, after the god of time. These allusions were the best our ancestors could do. They possessed no scientific instruments beyond the naked eye. They were confined to Earth and had no idea that it too is a planet.

When ancient scholars designed the week—a period of time with no intrinsic astronomical significance unlike the day, month, and year—they gave it seven days and named each after one of the seven anomalous lights in the night sky. We can readily make out the remnants of this convention. In the English language, Saturday is Saturn's day. Sunday and Monday are clear enough. Tuesday through Friday are named after the gods of the Saxon and Teutonic invaders of Celtic/Roman Britain. Wednesday, for example is Odin's (Wodin's) day; Thursday is Thor's day. Saturday came from the Romans, but the names of the other days have Germanic roots.

This collection of seven gods, seven days, and seven worlds—the Sun, Moon, and five wandering planets—entered the perceptions of people everywhere. The number seven began to acquire supernatural connotations. There were seven "heavens," the transparent spherical shells centered on Earth that were imagined to make these worlds move. The outermost, seventh heaven, was where the "fixed" stars were imagined to reside. There were seven days of creation (if we include God's day of rest), seven deadly sins, seven evil demons in Sumerian myth, seven vowels in the Greek alphabet (each affiliated with a planetary god), and seven alchemical "bodies" (gold, silver, iron, mercury, lead, tin, and copper, each associated with a planet). Seven is a lucky number. St. Augustine obscurely argued for the mystic importance of seven on the grounds that three "is the first whole number that is odd" (what about one?), "four the first that is even" (what about two?), and "of these . . . seven is composed." And so on. Even in our times, these associations linger.

Several centuries ago, people disbelieved Galileo's discovery of the four satellites of Jupiter—hardly planets—on the grounds that it challenged the precedence of the number seven. As acceptance of the Copernican system grew, the solar system had only six planets (Mercury, Venus, Earth, Mars, Jupiter, and Saturn). So learned academic arguments arose that explained why there had to be six. For example, six is the first "perfect" number, a number equal to the sum of its divisors $(1 + 2 + 3)$. And anyway, there were only six days of creation, not seven. People mystically accommodated from seven worlds to six.

As those adept at numerological mysticism adjusted to the Copernican system, this self-indulgent mode of thinking spilled over from planets to moons. Earth had one moon; Jupiter had the four Galilean moons. That made five. Clearly one was missing. (Don't forget: Six is the first perfect number.) The science historian I. Bernard Cohen of Harvard University has pointed out that after Huygens discovered Saturn's moon Titan in 1655, he actually gave up searching for other moons because it was apparent from such arguments that no more were to be found.

Sixteen years later, ironically with Huygens in attendance, Giovanni Cassini of the Paris Observatory discovered a seventh moon—Iapetus, a bizarre world circling Saturn outside of Titan's orbit. Shortly after, Cassini discovered Rhea, the Saturnian moon interior to Titan.

When astronomers made claims of new worlds in the late eighteenth century, the force of such numerological arguments had much dissipated. Still, it was with a real sense of surprise that people in 1781 heard about a new planet discovered through a telescope. New moons were comparatively unimpressive, especially after the first six or eight. That there were new planets to be found and that humans had devised the means to do so were both considered astonishing. If there is one previously unknown planet, there may be many more in this solar system and in others. Who can tell what might be found if a multitude of new worlds is hiding in the dark?

The discovery wasn't even made by a professional astronomer but by William Herschel, a musician whose relatives had come to Britain with the family of another anglicized German, the reigning monarch and future oppressor of the American colonists, George III. It became Herschel's wish to call the planet George ("George's Star," actually) after his patron but, providentially, the name didn't stick. Instead, the planet that Herschel found (he thought it was a comet at first) is called Uranus, after the ancient Greek sky god who was Saturn's father and thus the grandfather of the Olympian gods.

We no longer consider the Sun and Moon to be planets and count Uranus as the seventh planet in order from the Sun. The four outer, Jovian planets turn out to be very different from the four inner, terrestrial planets. Pluto is a separate case, fitting into neither category.

As the years passed and the quality of astronomical instruments improved, we began to learn more about distant Uranus. What reflects the dim sunlight back to us is no solid surface, but atmosphere and clouds—just as for Jupiter, Saturn, and Neptune. The air on Uranus is made of hydrogen and helium, the two simplest gases. Methane and other hydrocarbons are also present. Just below the clouds visible to Earthbound observers are enormous quantities of ammonia, hydrogen sulfide, and, especially, water.

Deep inside Jupiter and Saturn the pressures are so great that atoms sweat electrons and the air becomes a metal. That does not seem to happen on less massive Uranus because the pressures at depth are less. Still deeper inside Uranus, under the crushing weight of the overlying atmosphere, is a rocky surface—discovered only by its subtle tugs on the planet's moons and wholly inaccessible to view. A big Earth-like planet is hiding down there, swathed in an immense blanket of air.

Earth's surface temperature is due to the sunlight it intercepts. Turn off the Sun and the planet soon chills—not to trifling Antarctic cold, not just so cold that the oceans freeze, but to a cold so intense that the very air condenses, forming a 10-meter-thick layer of oxygen and nitrogen snows covering the whole planet. The little bit of energy that trickles out from Earth's hot interior would be insufficient to melt these snows. But for Jupiter, Saturn, and Neptune, it's different. Their interiors pour out about as much heat as their surfaces acquire from the warmth of the distant Sun. Turn off the Sun and they would be affected only a little.

But Uranus is different: Uranus is an anomaly among the Jovian planets. Uranus is like Earth, with very little intrinsic heat pouring out. We have no good understanding of why this should be—why Uranus, which in many respects is so similar to Neptune, should lack a potent source of internal heat.

Uranus is different in another way: It lies on its side as it goes around the Sun. During the 1990s, the south pole is heated by the Sun, and it is this pole that Earthbound observers see when they look at Uranus. It takes Uranus 84 Earth years to go around the Sun. So in the 2030s, the north pole will be Sunward (and Earthward). In the 2070s the south pole will be pointing to the Sun again. In between, Earthbound astronomers will be looking mainly at equatorial latitudes.

All the other planets spin much more upright in their orbits. No one is sure why Uranus spins anomalously. The most promising suggestion is that sometime in its early history, billions of years ago, it was struck by an Earth-sized rogue planet that was traveling in a highly eccentric orbit. Such a collision, if it happened, must have caused much tumult in the Uranus system. For all we know, there may be other vestiges of ancient havoc still left for us to find. But Uranus' remoteness tends to guard the planet's mysteries.

In 1977 a team of scientists led by James Elliot (then of Cornell University) accidentally discovered that Uranus, like Saturn, has rings. The scientists were flying over the Indian Ocean in a special NASA airplane, the Kuiper Airborne Observatory, to witness Uranus pass in front of, or occult, a distant star. The observers were surprised to find that the star winked on and off several times just before it passed behind Uranus and its atmosphere and then several times more just after it emerged. Because the patterns of winking on and off were the same before and after the occultation, this finding (and much subsequent work) has led to the discovery of nine thin, dark rings surrounding the planet, giving it the appearance of a bull's-eye in the sky.

Surrounding the rings, Earthbound astronomers understood, were the concentric orbits of the five moons then known: Miranda, Ariel, Umbriel, Titania, and Oberon. They're named after characters in Shakespeare's *A Midsummer Night's Dream* and *The Tempest* and in Alexander Pope's *The Rape of the Lock*. Two of them, Titania and Oberon, were found by Herschel himself. The innermost of the five, Miranda, was discovered as recently as 1948, by my teacher Gerard Kuiper. (He so named it because of the words spoken by Miranda, the heroine of *The Tempest*: "O brave new world, That has such people in't." To which Prospero replies, "'Tis new to thee." Just so. Like all other worlds in the solar system, Miranda is 4.5 billion years old.) I remember how great an achievement people back then considered the discovery of a new moon of Uranus.

A revolution in our understanding of the Uranus system—the planet, its rings, and moons—began on January 24, 1986. On that day, after a journey of 8 1/2 years, the Voyager 2 spacecraft sailed near Miranda. Uranus' gravity then flung the spacecraft on to Neptune. Voyager returned 4,300 close-up pictures of the Uranus system and a wealth of other data.

Planetary scientists found Uranus to be surrounded by an intense radiation belt, electrons and protons trapped by the planet's magnetic field. Voyager flew through this radiation belt, measuring the magnetic field and the trapped particles as it went. It also detected—in changing timbres, harmonies, and nuance, but mainly in fortissimo—a cacophony of radio waves generated by the speeding, trapped particles. Something similar exists at Jupiter, Saturn, and Neptune, but always with a theme and counterpoint characteristic of each world.

On Earth the magnetic and geographical poles are quite close together. On Uranus, the magnetic axis and the axis of rotation tilt away from each other by some 60 degrees. No one yet understands why. Some have suggested that we are catching Uranus in a reversal of its north and south magnetic poles, as periodically happens on Earth. Others propose that this too is the consequence of that mighty, ancient collision that knocked the planet over. But we do not know.

Among the principal glories of Voyager's encounter with Uranus were the pictures. With the two television cameras on the spacecraft, astronomers discovered 10 new moons, determined the length of the day in the clouds of Uranus (about 17 hours), and studied about a dozen rings. The most spectacular pictures were those returned from the five larger, previously known moons, especially the smallest of them, Kuiper's Miranda. Its surface is a tumult of fault valleys, parallel ridges, sheer cliffs, low mountains, impact craters, and frozen floods of once-molten surface material. This turmoiled landscape is unexpected in a small, cold, icy world so distant from the Sun.

Perhaps the surface was melted and reworked in some long-gone epoch when a gravitational resonance between Uranus, Miranda, and Ariel pumped energy from the planet into Miranda's interior. Or perhaps we are seeing the results of the primordial collision that may have knocked Uranus over. Or just conceivably, maybe a wild careening world utterly destroyed Miranda, dismembered it, and blasted it into smithereens, with many collision fragments still left in the moon's orbit. The shards and remnants, slowly colliding, gravitationally attracting each other, may have reaggregated into just such a jumbled, patchy, unfinished world as Miranda is today.

For me, there's something almost eerie about the pictures of dusky Miranda, because I can remember so well when it was only a faint point of light almost lost in the glare of Uranus, discovered through great difficulty by dint of the astronomer's skills and patience. In only half a lifetime it has gone from an undiscovered world to a destination, one whose ancient and idiosyncratic secrets have been at least partially revealed.

Reproduced by permission. © 2004 *Astronomy* magazine, Kalmbach Publishing Co.

Because Pluto is so far away, it appears very tiny to us here on Earth. Because it's so small, direct observations of Pluto are rare. However, when Pluto passed in front of a star in the summer of 2002, it was possible to make rare observations that revealed interesting information about what happens to that planet in its 248-year orbit around the Sun.

Giants in the Sky

Pluto's atmosphere appears to be experiencing global cooling, and data supports the idea that the surface seems to be warming up somewhat. This brief article talks about what the latest observations of Pluto have revealed.—EF

"Global Cooling Strikes Pluto"
by Vanessa Thomas
Astronomy, December 2002

Abstract: When Pluto passed in front of a star this summer, it confirmed suspicions that the distant planet's atmosphere changes during its 248-year journey around the Sun. The new observations, however, also suggest that the changes are even more drastic than imagined.

As solar system objects orbit the Sun, occasionally they pass between Earth and a star, an event known as an occultation. If the object has an atmosphere, astronomers can scrutinize the star's light just before and after the object blocks the star. Careful observations can reveal details about the density, temperature, and pressure of the object's atmosphere.

On July 19, Marc Buie of Arizona's Lowell Observatory set up a portable 14-inch telescope in northern Chile to watch Pluto occult a star called P126A. Because Pluto appears so small—its disk spans barely 0.1"—occultations are rare. The July event was the first one observed successfully since 1988. Afterward, Buie and James Elliot of the Massachusetts Institute of Technology compared the results of the two occultations.

"In the last 14 years, one or more changes have occurred," Buie says. "Pluto's atmosphere is undergoing global cooling, while other data indicate that the surface seems to be getting slightly warmer. Some change is inevitable as Pluto moves away from the Sun, but what we're seeing is more complex than expected."

From the earlier occultation and other observations, planetary scientists learned that Pluto has a thin atmosphere with nitrogen and some methane and carbon dioxide. In 1988, the occulted star's light dipped slightly at first before plunging sharply. This unexpected behavior suggested that Pluto's atmosphere could have a smog layer, or the temperature drops suddenly near the planet's surface.

In contrast, the July event provided a much smoother light curve, suggesting the cause of the abrupt drop witnessed in 1988 is no longer present. Additionally, the recent results show that Pluto's atmosphere has cooled between 20 [degrees] and 55 [degrees] Fahrenheit.

"A 1997 Triton occultation revealed that the surface of Triton, Neptune's largest moon, had warmed since the Voyager spacecraft first explored the moon in 1989," Elliot says. "But the changes seen in Pluto's atmosphere are much more severe."

"We cannot fully explain what has caused these dramatic changes to Pluto's atmosphere," Buie adds. "A mission to Pluto is our best hope for putting all the puzzle pieces together."

For years, NASA has included a spacecraft to Pluto in its plans, but budget problems have repeatedly delayed the mission. Last year, the U.S. Congress awarded a modest amount of funding to begin developing the New Horizons mission to Pluto, its moon, and the Kuiper Belt, but future financial support remains uncertain.

Reproduced by permission. © 2004 *Astronomy* magazine, Kalmbach Publishing Co.

Why are Uranus and Neptune so far from the Sun? They orbit at nineteen and thirty astronomical units respectively, rather than within ten astronomical units like the first six planets. Given the composition of these planets, scientists don't believe they could have formed naturally at their present locations.

The planets were created from hunks of primordial matter in a nebular disk of dust and gas. Larger pieces of matter collided until the planets were formed. However, on the edges of the nebula, matter was spread too thinly to form planets. The implication is that Neptune and Uranus were formed closer to the Sun and a subsequent event forced them to the outer edge of the solar system. A recent computer model has shed new light upon how the interaction of Uranus and Neptune with Saturn and Jupiter may have resulted in their current orbits.—EF

"Shaking Up a Nursery of Giant Planets"
by Richard A. Kerr
Science, **December 10, 1999**

What are Uranus and Neptune doing so far from the
sun? The question has puzzled theorists for decades.
Unlike the closest six planets, which orbit the sun
inside of 10 astronomical units (AU)—that is, less than
10 times farther out than Earth—Uranus and Neptune
orbit at 19 and 30 AU, respectively. Theorists don't
believe they could have formed so far out; there, gas
and dust were too sparse to coalesce into planets. Now,
a new computer model suggests that sibling rivalry
might be to blame for their banishment. Runty Uranus
and Neptune may have grown up in tight quarters
much closer to the sun, only to have the big bruisers
Jupiter and Saturn fling them into the outer reaches of
the solar system.

"It's a fascinating result," says planetary dynamicist
Brett Gladman of the Observatory of Nice in France. "I
think it's marvelous it works." Forming Neptune and
Uranus where it's practicable and then having them
thrown outward "seems dynamically plausible," adds
Stuart Weidenschilling of the Planetary Science
Institute in Tucson, Arizona. "It certainly comes out
ahead of any previous explanations."

The nine planets formed in a nebular disk of dust
and gas, where chunks of primordial matter collided to
form bigger and bigger chunks and eventually planets.
For the next several million years, the resulting ice-rock
cores of the outer planets grabbed gas from the nebula

until the gas was all taken up or blown away by the sun. But out on the nebula's fringes, matter was spread too thinly for anything like planets to form. In the best simulations of the process, cores for Uranus and Neptune fail to form at their present positions in even 4.5 billion years, the lifetime of the solar system. "Things just grow too slowly" in the outermost solar system, says Weidenschilling. "We've tried to form Uranus and Neptune at their present locations and failed miserably."

Apparently, Uranus and Neptune formed somewhere else, presumably closer to the sun where the nebula was far denser. But how did they move outward billions of kilometers without disrupting their nicely circular orbits, which are in the same plane as the rest of the solar system? In this week's issue of Nature, planetary dynamicists Edward Thommes and Martin Duncan of Queen's University in Kingston, Ontario, and Harold Levison of the Boulder, Colorado, branch of the Southwest Research Institute demonstrate a two-step method that works, at least in their model. They assume that not just two but four or five ice-rock cores formed where Jupiter and Saturn now reside, between 5 and 10 AU—an assumption most theorists are comfortable with.

Conventional thinking also has it that once a core reached a critical mass—about 15 times that of Earth—it would grow faster and faster as its increasing mass gave it greater and greater gravitational pull on the gas. By chance, in Thommes and Duncan's scenarios, Jupiter hit runaway growth first, letting it grab 71% of the total mass of the outer planets; Saturn came in second with 21%, but late bloomers Uranus and Neptune got only about 3% and 4% of the mass, respectively, leaving them at the mercy of nearby Jupiter and Saturn. In the first 100,000 years of many of the simulations, Jupiter and Saturn gravitationally fling their nursery mates into steeply tilted, highly elongated orbits that can carry them 30 or 40 AU outward.

That's a dangerous situation for an undersized giant because the big guys could, and in some of the simulations do, eject a planet from the solar system entirely. But the debris remaining in the disk, which extends to 40 AU and beyond, can step in to defend the bullied planets. In a process called dynamical friction, innumerable gravitational interactions with bits of disk debris push Uranus and Neptune around as they pass through and over the disk. The dynamical friction eases the wildly orbiting planets once again into circular orbits in the plane of the other planets but beyond the disruptive influence of Jupiter and Saturn. Further planet-disk interactions can move the relocated planets even farther out. Of the 24 simulations Thommes and his colleagues have run, about half produced an outer solar system resembling ours. Most runs also leave a disk of debris beyond 40 AU that closely resembles the Kuiper Belt of icy objects discovered in 1992, beyond the mean orbital distance of Pluto.

"It's a very interesting idea," says Jack J. Lissauer of NASA's Ames Research Center in Mountain View, California. "They've shown it's not as unlikely as I would have thought." But he and others question the realism of the model and note that no one is sure what the earliest solar system was actually like. Lissauer wonders, for example, if the modelers haven't put a bit too much debris in the outer solar system. Renu Malhotra of the Lunar and Planetary Institute in Houston believes cores would have interacted with gas and ice-rock bodies in the giant planet nursery where they formed. Such interactions, which don't appear in the model, would "tend to damp this violent physics" of throwing Uranus and Neptune out. "Whether the modeling reflects what happens in nature is not demonstrated," she says.

More realism will require more complicated modeling and more computing power, says Duncan. In the meantime, astronomers are pushing their telescopes to the limits to catch a glimpse of more-distant Kuiper Belt objects. In many of Thommes's simulations, Neptune scatters these objects high and low before settling down itself. Like debris from a brawl, scattered Kuiper Belt objects would be a strong sign that the giant planets had an early falling out.

Reprinted with permission from Richard A. Kerr, "Shaking Up a Nursery of Giant Planets," SCIENCE 286:2054. Copyright 1999 AAAS.

5 At the Edge of the Solar System

Pluto is smaller than Earth's moon. Comparable to an icy dwarf star, its composition is different from that of the other eight planets in the solar system. It is neither rocky like Earth, Venus, Mars, and Mercury, nor gaseous like Jupiter, Saturn, Uranus, and Neptune. In comparison to the other planets, it has a seventeen-degree tilt in its orbit. In fact, Pluto is a very strange planet—or, perhaps it is not a planet at all. Some scientists argue that Pluto isn't a legitimate planet but rather a very large Kuiper Belt object. Others, who defend Pluto's status as a planet, refer to the fact that Pluto possesses a moon unlike other bodies in the Kuiper Belt. This was thought to be a unique occurrence until 2001. This was when a group of astronomers headed by Christian Veillet of the Canada-France-Hawaii Telescope in Mauna Kea, Hawaii, discovered evidence that another Kuiper Belt object, called 1998 [W.sub.31], has a satellite.

Another justification for Pluto's status as a planet is that it is significantly larger than

groups in which astronomers classify the other planets. It isn't rocky like the so-called terrestrials—Mercury, Venus, Earth, and Mars. Nor is it one of the gas giants—like Jupiter, Saturn, Uranus, and Neptune. Pluto's icy composition resembles that of a comet.

That's why some scientists have argued for years that Pluto isn't a planet at all. Rather, they say, Pluto is an unusually large comet whose true family lies within the Kuiper belt, an outpost of icy objects beyond the orbit of Neptune. Since 1992, when astronomers spied the first object in the belt (SN: 9/26/92, p. 142), 377 have been found. This includes a group of four dubbed Plutinos because, like Pluto, their orbit has a special synchrony with that of Neptune. Every time Neptune goes around the sun three times, Pluto and the Plutinos go around twice.

Two new reports add to the mounting evidence that Pluto may be the king of the Kuiper belt rather than the pipsqueak of planets.

Researchers wanting to preserve Pluto's planetary status had noted that the body was the only denizen of the outer solar system known to possess a moon. Astronomers now report, however, that a card-carrying member of the Kuiper belt, a large comet-like object dubbed 1998 [W.sub.31], also has a moon.

Reviewing images of 1998 [W.sub.31] that they had taken last December, astronomers led by Christian Veillet of the Canada-France-Hawaii Telescope in Mauna Kea, Hawaii, found that the icy object was accompanied by a dimmer companion. Images taken by another team nearly a year earlier also show evidence of a satellite, Veillet and his collaborators report in an April 15 circular of the International Astronomical Union (IAU). They estimate that the moon lies at least 40,000 kilometers from 1998 [W.sub.31], about a tenth the distance between Earth and its moon.

In the IAU circular, Veillet and his colleagues pull no punches about how they classify Pluto. They say their finding "indicates that 1998 [W.sub.31] is the second [member of the Kuiper belt] to have a satellite (after Pluto)."

In the May 24 NATURE, astronomers trounce another possible objection to a Plutonian association with the Kuiper belt—the body's large size relative to known belt members. David Jewitt and Herve Aussel of the University of Hawaii in Honolulu, with Aaron Evans of the State University of New York at Stony Brook, monitored a recently discovered Kuiper belt object, known as (20000) Varuna.

Observing Varuna in both visible light and in submillimeter wavelengths, Jewitt's team determined that Varuna has a diameter of about 900 km. That's roughly 40 percent the diameter of Pluto and only slightly less than that of Pluto's moon Charon.

"The results suggest that Pluto and Charon are not uniquely large objects [in the outer solar system] and that a continuum of sizes may exist," say Stephen C. Tegler and William Romanishin, both of the University of Oklahoma in Norman, in a commentary accompanying the NATURE report.

"We can now imagine that bodies even larger and more distant than Pluto will be found," the commenters note.

"I think findings over the past few years put the last nails in the Pluto-the-planet coffin," declares Brian G. Marsden of the Harvard-Smithsonian Center for Astrophysics in Cambridge, Mass.

Some astronomers argue that the whole debate is a waste of time, having to do with semantics and not science. Still, the controversy continues. In 1999, the IAU decided not to reclassify Pluto as a denizen of the Kuiper belt (SN: 2/27/99, p. 139). Yet, many astronomers concede that if Pluto had been discovered yesterday rather than in 1930, it probably wouldn't be called a planet.

Marsden notes that in 1801, when astronomers spied a large chunk of rock called Ceres, they called it a planet. As more and more such rocks turned up, scientists reclassified Ceres as a member of the asteroid belt occupying the region between the orbits of Mars and Jupiter. Ceres remains the largest asteroid known, but no one doubts it's an asteroid, Marsden adds.

When the American Museum of Natural History's Rose Center for Earth and Space opened last year in New York, it became clear that Neil deGrasse Tyson, director of the museum's planetarium, had taken a quiet but firm stance on the Pluto controversy. One of the displays has these words: "Beyond the outer planets is the Kuiper Belt of comets, a disk of small, icy worlds including Pluto." When the New York Times publicized that statement, it caused an uproar.

"More power to him!" says Marsden about de-Grasse Tyson's decision. Giving Pluto a dual status as both the smallest planet and the largest Kuiper belt member, or even stripping it of its planethood, is not a demotion, insists Marsden.

"It's still an interesting object," he says. "It's just that it's an interesting member of the Kuiper belt."

SCIENCE NEWS by Ron Cowen. Copyright 2001 by SCI SERVICE INC. Reproduced with permission of SCI SERVICE INC in the textbook format via Copyright Clearance Center.

Is Pluto the last major planet in our solar system? Is Pluto a planet at all? More than 600 objects have been found in the Kuiper Belt in the last decade. However, the discovery in 2002 of Quaoar, the largest Kuiper Belt object, half the size of Pluto, by two Caltech astronomers, Michael E. Brown and Chadwick A. Trujillo, is the most interesting. In addition to interest in the Quaoar itself, the discovery of a Kuiper Belt object that is not much smaller than Pluto and that has a more regular orbit has added fuel to the controversy over whether Pluto should legitimately be considered a major planet or as just a large Kuiper Belt object. More important, however, the nature and orbits of planetlike objects such as Quaoar in the Kuiper Belt provide fascinating information about the formation of the planets in our solar system and Earth itself.—EF

"Tightening Our Kuiper Belt: From the Edge of the Solar System Come Hints of a Disrupted Youth"
by Charles Liu
Natural History, February 2003

More and more often, some new astronomical discovery is thrusting Pluto and its home, the Kuiper Belt, into the public eye. Most of the attention focuses on Pluto's status as one of our solar system's major planets. Should it retain that status, even though astronomers know Pluto really is just a ball of ice and rock, smaller than our Moon?

A few months ago the flames were fanned again, when Michael E. Brown and Chadwick A. Trujillo, both astronomers at Caltech, announced the discovery of a large new Kuiper Belt object (or KBO) that they dubbed Quaoar (after the creation force of the Tonga tribe who lived in the Los Angeles area). No one was calling Quaoar a major planet; it's only 800 miles wide. Yet Pluto—about 1,400 miles in diameter—isn't that much bigger than Quaoar, and Quaoar's orbit looks much more like the orbits of the other eight major planets than Pluto's does. Pluto-bashers everywhere hailed Quaoar as further proof that the runt of the traditional nine planets should be reclassified as just another KBO, albeit a large one.

But all the hoopla missed the scientific point. For many of us astronomers, it's not Pluto, Quaoar, or any other individual KBO that matters; it's the Kuiper Belt itself that counts. And if you take the Pluto-Quaoar episode as an occasion for a closer look at the Kuiper

Belt, you get into some pretty intriguing scientific questions. For example, R. Lynne Allen of the University of British Columbia in Vancouver and her collaborators recently published findings that, though useless to the argument about what to call Pluto, suggest that the Kuiper Belt is a surprisingly sharp edge cinching our solar system five billion miles out from the Sun, and that it holds some clues to our solar system's early history.

Named after the Dutch American astronomer Gerard Kuiper, one of the first people to posit its existence, the Kuiper Belt is a doughnut-shaped zone of space, populated by comets and comet-like bodies, which lies beyond the orbit of Neptune. KBOs are small—most are less than 100 miles across—and made up almost entirely of ice and rock. They're remnants of the solar system's early history, relatively unaltered by four and a half billion years of stellar and planetary evolution.

Someday astronomers will get the chance to study KBOs up close, and the objects will provide an unparalleled glimpse into the chemical and physical conditions of the early solar system. But the scientific value of the Kuiper Belt as a whole is even greater than the sum of the information in every icy dirt ball. The reason is that in the past decade or so, astronomers have discovered disks of dusty gas as large as 100 billion miles in diameter orbiting a number of stars much younger than, but otherwise quite similar to, our Sun. According to current astrophysical models, planets originate in these disks, and our solar system represents one possible outcome of the evolution of such a disk. The Kuiper Belt is probably what remains of the Sun's original disk, so its shape, size, and thickness serve as critical benchmarks for understanding how planetary systems form, grow, and age.

Neptune's orbit, a nearly circular ellipse some three billion miles away from the Sun, traces the Kuiper Belt's inner edge. The belt's outer edge is far less certain, though. Of more than 600 KBOs discovered to date, none of those with nearly circular orbits is more than roughly five billion miles from the Sun. That suggests the Kuiper Belt's outer boundary could well lie there. But the outer boundaries of the disks orbiting the younger stars I mentioned are as much as twenty times farther away from their central stars. If the Kuiper Belt is what's left of such a disk around our Sun, why is it so small?

To resolve this discrepancy, astronomers have proposed a composite shape for the Kuiper Belt, with an inner part that bulges like a bagel, and an outer part that's thin like a dinner plate. According to that model, the belt extends a long way out, but the hypothetical KBOs that would allegedly make up the outer part of the belt haven't been discovered because they're confined to a narrow band—about the width of an outstretched pinkie—across the sky.

Enter Lynne Allen. To test the predictions of the model, she trained the four-meter telescope at the Kitt Peak National Observatory in Arizona on portions of the band of sky where the model suggested she would find the outer Kuiper Belt. Sure enough, she found dozens of new KBOs there to be sure, but none of them were more than five billion miles away. By Allen's calculations, the observations strongly suggest that the

KBO distribution has a sharp boundary at that distance, and that a thin outer Kuiper Belt simply does not exist.

So the question remains: why is the Sun's Kuiper Belt so much smaller than the disks of other stars? One possibility is that, billions of years ago, our solar system suffered a major disturbance—perhaps a near-collision with a passing star—that chopped the outer regions off the Sun's circumstellar disk. If so, such a cropping would have directly affected the development of our entire planetary system. For one thing, a larger disk might have caused many more comet collisions early in Earth's history. If the passing-star scenario can be confirmed, it may show that the development of life on Earth was linked to a chance but crucial event in the history of the Kuiper Belt.

Reprinted from *Natural History* February 2003; copyright © *Natural History* Magazine, Inc. 2003.

When it was discovered in 1930, tiny Pluto was declared to be the ninth planet, a finding that was accepted for decades. Planets were clearly bodies in space different from tiny objects such as asteroids and enormous ones like stars. In the 1990s, however, scientists began discovering new types of objects in space. Among these new objects were icy bodies in the same region of space where Pluto dwelled, and some of these were half the size of Pluto. Suddenly, Pluto's status as a planet began to be questioned.

Before scientists can come up with a definitive answer to whether or not Pluto is a planet, they must first agree on what a planet is. Some astronomers proposed that any object with a moon should qualify. Others suggested that only objects with an atmosphere should be considered planets. Still others wanted a definition based on size.

In 1999 and 2000, members of the International Astronomical Union hotly discussed this topic. This article describes the presently accepted definition of what a planet is and what the implications of this new definition are.—EF

"Is Pluto a Planet?"
by Alan Stern
Odyssey, April 2002

Pluto is a small world, only 2,400 km in diameter. Ever since its discovery in 1930, it has been considered the ninth planet. Recently, however, its planetary status has been challenged. Should Pluto be considered a planet? To fully answer this question, we must examine what it even means to be a planet.

Until the 1990s, the subject of what it means to be a planet was not actively considered by scientists. Why? Because the only planets known were the ones in our solar system, and these nine bodies seemed sufficiently different from both smaller bodies (like asteroids and comets) and larger ones (like stars) that there really was no need for a formal definition to be developed.

However, in the 1990s, astronomers detected new kinds of bodies in space that significantly blurred the situation. These new kinds of objects included super-size planets much more massive than Jupiter, and some failed stars (called brown dwarfs, objects that could not sustain the fires of nuclear fusion for very long) much larger than super-planets but much smaller and cooler than any star. The new objects also included hundreds of small, icy bodies in the same distant region of the solar system as Pluto, each hundreds of kilometers across—some half as large as Pluto!

With these discoveries, astronomers and laypeople alike started to ask: Just exactly what is a planet? Some astronomers proposed that any object with a moon should be considered a planet. But this definition leaves out the planets Mercury and Venus, and worse, some asteroids were then discovered to have moons of their own.

Other astronomers proposed that perhaps planet-hood should imply that an object has an atmosphere. But Mercury's atmosphere is so thin that few astronomers even consider it a real one, and Pluto's atmosphere comes and goes every time Pluto orbits the sun. Clearly, this criterion had problems.

Some astronomers wanted to exclude objects that were not primarily made of rock or gas. But most astronomers considered it arbitrary to exclude icy bodies. (This didn't affect Pluto's status. Pluto is known to have an icy covering, but to be about 70 percent composed of rocky material; the other 30 percent is ice.)

Other astronomers suggested a simple definition, based only on a minimum and maximum size—say, larger than 1,000 kilometers across and smaller than 100,000 kilometers. But this had problems, too. For one thing, it was unpopular with many scientists because it was so arbitrary. For another, although all nine of the planets in our solar system fit this definition, so would white dwarf stars!

Clearly, something better was needed—something that fit with common sense, and, at the same time, would be based on physics. What astronomers wanted was a definition that would admit most or all of the planets in our solar system and the solar systems being discovered around other stars, while at the same time excluding white dwarfs, rocks, boulders, burned-out stars, and other obviously non-planetary bodies. Most astronomers also wanted a definition that would allow them to classify an object either as a planet or not as a planet, based on observations that could be made today of the object. These observations included its size or mass or another physical attribute (but not, for example, based on how it was formed, which cannot be determined uniquely from telescopic observations). And most astronomers wanted the definition to be based on the object in question, as opposed, for example, to its location in a solar system, or whether the object orbited near other similar bodies. (As one astronomer put it, "We don't classify animals into species based on what other animals they are near, we classify them based on genetics. Let's find something genetic that represents planethood.")

Thus, although Pluto would be considered a planet by any of the definitions proposed above (it has a moon; it has an atmosphere; it's larger than 1,000 kilometers in diameter), a more general definition was needed that could be applied outside our own solar system.

What did they come up with instead? In 1999 and 2000, various members of the International Astronomical Union debated this topic via e-mail, in scientific meetings, and in print. The "solution," which is today widely (but not universally) accepted, is this: A planetary body would be any object that fits two criteria. First, it must be too small to generate nuclear fusion in its interior, as stars and brown dwarfs do. Second, it must be large enough to have its shape be controlled by gravity, rather than the strength of the materials (rocks, ice, etc.) of which it is made. This second criterion in essence means that the object must be nearly spherical due to the force of gravity; further, it eliminates rocks, boulders, and all of the small asteroids and comets. It is this genetic quality that signifies planethood (after all, all kids know how to draw a planet—you begin by drawing a circle), just as generating energy by nuclear fusion is the genetic quality that is the hallmark of all stars.

Together, the two criteria just described nicely allow all of the nine planets you are taught about in school to be considered planets. However, this new definition is richer than just that, allowing a much broader range of objects to be classified as planetary bodies, too.

For one thing, the two criteria described above allow (indeed, even insist that) large, planet-size moons be considered planetary bodies. For that reason, most astronomers now like to distinguish between planetary bodies (objects that meet the two criteria outlined above) and planets (objects that are the subset of planetary bodies and that orbit around a star—and not some other planet).

For another thing, the definition of planethood described above also allows many of the largest asteroids and Kuiper Belt objects to be considered planets. For this reason, it is increasingly common to hear planetary astronomers refer to various classes of planets, such as gas giants, ice giants, terrestrial (roughly Earth-size) worlds, and dwarf planets.

Although this situation is more complex than textbooks taught as little as a decade ago, it far better reflects the reality of what nature has produced, both in our solar system and in others. So, too, it also reflects the growing maturity of planetary science, which now recognizes that there are many "shades of gray" in science, just as there are in our lives.

It would be dishonest to say that all astronomers agree with the thinking outlined above. This reflects honest differences of opinion among scientists grappling with the new discoveries being made in our solar systems and in others. Nevertheless, most astronomers consider Pluto to be a planet (more specifically, an ice dwarf planet). This is probably best reflected by the decision of the International Astronomical Union in 1999, after much debate and consideration, to continue to classify Pluto as such.

From ODYSSEY'S April 2002 issue: Planets X © 2002, Cobblestone Publishing, 30 Grove Street, Suite C, Petersborough, NH 03458. All Rights Reserved. Reprinted by permission of Carus Publishing Company.

One of the most exciting discoveries in the past decade has been the discovery that planets exist that orbit stars other than our own Sun. In 1992, astronomers discovered the first planet outside our own solar system, orbiting a burned-out star. Then, in 1995, Swiss scientists found the first planet orbiting a Sun-like star in the constellation Pegasus. Since then, more than 100 planets have been identified. As recently as 2003, scientists announced the discovery of the most distant planet yet discovered, located more than 5,000 light-years from Earth. This is thirty times as far away as the next-farthest-away planet discovered. Such discoveries are helping scientists understand the planets such as Saturn and Jupiter in our own solar system. This article looks at how our current knowledge about the composition of planets in our own solar system can help us identify new planets and what new information about new

*planets can tell us about the formation of planets
in our own solar system.—EF*

"Search for More Worlds Expands as Astronomers Add Data, Techniques"
**by Alexandra Witze
Knight Ridder/Tribune News Service
January 27, 2003**

SEATTLE—Gene Roddenberry and Isaac Asimov always knew there were other worlds out there. And now astronomers agree.

Just last week, scientists added the 105th entry to their list of planets beyond the solar system. These are bizarre places: big, gassy balls like Jupiter, including at least one orbiting so close to a star that it's hot enough to vaporize iron.

Even Klingons wouldn't want to live on these worlds. But scientists can't wait to find out more about them.

New discoveries, including the recent announcement of the most distant planet known, are helping astronomers understand the weird new worlds. Soon, scientists think, they may even achieve the long-sought goal of discovering a small, rocky planet like our own.

"We stand on the verge of being able to find planets like Earth," Melissa McGrath, an astronomer at the Space Telescope Science Institute in Baltimore, said during a recent meeting in Seattle.

For centuries, scholars have wondered whether planets orbit the billions of other stars in the Milky Way. Today, planet discoveries are flooding in so quickly that textbooks are constantly outdated.

Scientists have discovered a story more vivid, more wonderful than anything Ray Bradbury could have invented.

"When this is done," says astronomer Dimitar Sasselov, "we will achieve what happens only once in many generations—understanding what is our place in the universe."

The prologue to this story came in 1992, when astronomers discovered a planet orbiting a pulsar—a burned-out, rapidly rotating star emitting lethal amounts of radiation. The main tale began in 1995, when Swiss researchers announced the first planet around a sunlike star, 51 Pegasi in the constellation Pegasus.

An exciting chapter was added this month with the announcement of the most distant extrasolar planet known.

That newfound world lies 5,000 light-years from Earth, more than 30 times the previous record for most distant planet. Astronomers made that leap of light-years using a new planet-hunting technique that takes advantage of eclipses.

Just as the moon eclipses the sun when it passes between the sun and Earth, so do extrasolar planets sometimes eclipse their stars. As seen from Earth, the eclipse is tiny, like the outline of a flea crawling across a spotlight. But astronomers can catch an eclipse, or "transit," by monitoring the light of thousands of stars.

Astronomers calculate that about one in every 3,000 stars might have a planet in just the right orientation to be observed. By watching the light of enough stars, scientists hope to see an eclipse in progress, thus revealing the presence of a planet that would be too small to photograph.

That's how a team led by Maciej Konacki of the California Institute of Technology discovered the distant planet around a star known as OGLE-TR-56.

The researchers used data gathered by a Polish-American project known as OGLE, or Optical Gravitational Lensing Experiment, which uses a telescope in Chile to monitor the brightness of more than 50,000 stars. The scientists came up with a list of candidates that may be undergoing eclipses.

OGLE-TR-56 was the 56th such transit candidate. Its light dimmed regularly every 29 hours, suggesting the presence of a close-in planet.

The scientists confirmed the discovery with four nights' observation at the world's largest telescope, the Keck telescope in Hawaii. There they found that the light from OGLE-TR-56 did in fact vary in a way consistent with the presence of a planet—shifting slightly bluer, then redder, as the star moved slightly toward and away from Earth under the planet's gravitational influence.

That star-jiggle technique, known formally as the radial velocity method, has been the primary way of finding the other hundred extrasolar planets so far. But the new discovery shows that transits may be an easier and faster way to scout for planets, said Dr. Sasselov, who was part of the research team. Only a few nights of follow-up are needed to confirm a given find with the radial velocity method.

In addition, the radial velocity method can detect only planets around nearby stars, within a few hundred light-years. The transit method could conceivably reach out 8,000 light-years, said Dr. Sasselov. (One light-year equals about 6 trillion miles.)

"Today we know it works," he said in Seattle this month at a meeting of the American Astronomical Society. "It opens the door for the discovery of many more."

He's not the only one thrilled.

"This is a big step forward in this field," says Sara Seager of the Carnegie Institution of Washington. "It's the beginning of a new wave of extrasolar planets."

More than 20 transit searches are now under way. "There's a piece of the sky for everyone," she says.

Transit searches are also important because they can yield relatively accurate estimates of the masses and sizes of extrasolar planets. That information, in turn, confirms that they are low-density gas giants like Jupiter. And that conclusion, Dr. Seager says, helps astronomers better define their ideas of how stars and planets are born and evolve.

For instance, most astronomers think that giant planets probably form far out from their stars, then spiral in to orbit closer than Mercury does to the sun. Our solar system, with the gas giants Jupiter and Saturn so far out, may be an anomaly.

So scientists are trying to study the new planets with the open-mindedness of a science-fiction writer.

New data, however, are starting to limit visions of what such planets could be like, including how their temperatures change seasonally and how gases circulate in their atmospheres. So far, scientists have measured the atmosphere on one extrasolar planet by watching its light during a transit.

Turning that around, astronomers have imagined what Earth would look like if seen from afar. The big question: If aliens were looking at Earth, how would they know life existed here?

Earth's atmosphere, it turns out, is very different from its lifeless neighbors Venus and Mars, says Dr. Seager. For instance, ozone and oxygen molecules exist here, which suggests that there must be some continuous source of oxygen.

Astronomers hope they will be able to recognize similar signs of life on extrasolar planets.

NASA has grand plans for this quest. In 2006, it plans to launch Kepler, a telescope that will search for transits from space. Around 2015, Kepler's follow-up, the Terrestrial Planet Finder, is also slated for launch. Terrestrial Planet Finder, or TPF, would search for Earthlike planets and study their atmospheres for any signs of life.

"It's been said that all roads lead to TPF," says Dr. Seager. The European Space Agency is working on a similar project, called Darwin, for launch around the same time.

She predicted that by 2010, astronomers will have found the first Earthlike planets and enter a new wave of understanding.

"These," she says, "are very exciting times."

Reprinted with permission from Knight Ridder/Tribune (KRT) and TMS Reprints.

Web Sites

Due to the changing nature of Internet links, the Rosen Publishing Group, Inc., has developed an online list of Web sites related to the subject of this book. This site is updated regularly. Please use this link to access the list:

http://www.rosenlinks.com/cdfa/scsfp

For Further Reading

Beebe, Reta. *Jupiter: The Giant Planet* (Smithsonian Library of the Solar System). Washington, DC: Smithsonian Books, 1997.

Boyce, Joseph M. *The Smithsonian Book of Mars* (Smithsonian Library of the Solar System). Washington, DC: Smithsonian Books, 2003.

Cattermole, Peter John. *Mars: The Mystery Unfolds.* New York, NY: Oxford University Press, 2001.

Fischer, Daniel. *Mission Jupiter: The Spectacular Journey of the* Galileo *Spacecraft.* New York, NY: Copernicus Books, 2001.

Hartmann, William K. *A Traveler's Guide to Mars: The Mysterious Landscapes of the Red Planet.* New York, NY: Workman Publishing, 2003.

Henbest, Nigel. *The Planets: Portraits of New Worlds.* New York, NY: Penguin Books, 1994.

Hunt, Garry E., and Patrick Moore. *Atlas of Uranus.* New York, NY: Cambridge University Press, 1989.

Lang, Kenneth R. *The Cambridge Guide to the Solar System.* New York, NY: Cambridge University Press, 2003.

McNab, David, and James Younger. *The Planets.* New Haven, CT: Yale University Press, 1999.

Bibliography

Berman, Bob. "Sky Lights: Colors Reveal What's Brewing on Other Planets." *Discover*, Vol. 22, No. 12, December 2001.

Burnham, Robert. "Into the Maelstrom." *Astronomy*, Vol. 24, No. 4, April 1996, p. 42.

Cowen, Ron. "Nine Planets, or Eight?" *Science News*, Vol. 159, No. 23, June 9, 2001, p. 360.

Durisen, Richard H. "Planetary Rings: Moonlets in a Cosmic Sandblaster." *Mercury*, Vol. 28, No. 5, September 1999, p. 10.

Esposito, Larry. "Cassini Imaging at Jupiter." *Science*, Vol. 299, No. 5612, March 7, 2003, p. 1529.

Golombek, Matthew P. "The Surface of Mars: Not Just Dust and Rocks." *Science*, Vol. 300 No. 5628, June 27, 2003, p. 2043.

Grinspoon, David H. "Venus Unveiled: A Great Volcanic Flood Must Have Resurfaced Earth's Sister World Some 600 Million Years Ago." *Astronomy*, Vol. 25, No. 5, May 1997, p. 44.

Kerr, Richard A. "Shaking Up a Nursery of Giant Planets." *Science*, Vol. 286, No. 5447, December 10, 1999, p. 2054.

Kluger, Jeffrey. "The Blueberries of Mars: Was the Red Planet Once a Wet Planet?" *Time*, Vol. 163, March 15, 2004, p. 74.

Kluger, Jeffrey. "Secrets of the Rings: What Cassini Discovered When It Got to Saturn—and the Wonders It May Uncover in the Mission to Come." *Time*, Vol. 164, No. 2, July 12, 2004, p. 52.

Liu, Charles. "Tightening Our Kuiper Belt: From the Edge of the Solar System Come Hints of a Disrupted Youth." *Natural History*, Vol. 112, February 2003, p. 66.

Morton, Oliver. "Don't Ignore the Planet Next Door." *Science*, Vol. 298, No. 5599, November 29, 2002, p. 1706.

Motazedian, Tahirih. "Does Mars Have Flowing Water?" *Astronomy*, Vol. 32, No. 6, June 2004, p. 66.

Panek, Richard. "Rings Around the Planets." *Natural History*, Vol. 109, No. 8, October 2000, p. 32.

Ravilious, Kate. "Did Lava Cover Traces of Asteroid Impacts?" *New Scientist*, Vol. 176, No. 2373, December 14, 2002, p. 16.

Robinson, Mark S. and Paul G. Lucey. "Recalibrated Mariner 10 Color Mosaics: Implications for Mercurian Volcanism." *Science*, Vol. 275, No. 5297, January 10, 1997, p. 197.

Rubin, Alan. "Exposing Saturn's Secrets." *Astronomy*, Vol. 30, No. 12, December 2002, p. 49.

Sagan, Carl. "The First New Planet." *Astronomy*, Vol. 23, No. 3, March 1995, p. 34.

Samuel, Eugenie. "By Jove! If You Go Down to the Planet's Core, You're Sure of a Big Surprise." *New Scientist*, Vol. 174, No. 2340, April 27, 2002, p. 9.

Schilling, Govert. "Moon Behaving Badly: Why Won't Two of Saturn's Satellites Obey the Rules?" *New Scientist*, Vol. 174, No. 2337, April 6, 2002, p. 38.

Science News Staff. "The Importance of Being Jupiter." Vol. 147, No. 7, February 18, 1995, p. 111.

Spudis, Paul D. "How Earth Got its Moon." *Astronomy*, Vol. 32, No. 7, July 2004, p. 42.

Stern, Alan. "Is Pluto a Planet?" *Odyssey*, Vol. 11, No. 4, April 2002, p.14.

Stern, S. Alan. "Into the Outer Limits: Astronomers Are Figuring out How the Edgeworth-Kuiper Belt Formed and Evolved." *Astronomy*, Vol. 28, No. 9, September 2000, p. 52.

Thomas, Vanessa. "Global Cooling Strikes Pluto." *Astronomy*, Vol. 30, No. 12, December 2002, p. 22.

Weiss, Peter. "Land Before Time." *Earth*, Vol. 7, No. 1, February 1998,p. 28.

Witze, Alexandra. "Search for More Worlds Expands as Astronomers Add Data, Techniques." Knight Ridder/Tribune News Service, January 27, 2003, p. K7951.

Index

About the Editor

Ellen Foxxe has a B.A. from Harvard University and extensive experience working in the high technology field. She has two science-fiction novels to her credit. She divides her time between New Orleans and Boston.

Photo Credits

Front cover (top inset) © Royalty-Free/Corbis; (center left inset) © Digital Vision/Getty Images; (bottom right inset) © Getty Images/Taxi; (bottom left inset) © Library of Congress Prints and Photographs Division; (background) Brand X Pictures/Getty Images. Back cover (top) © Photodisc Green/Getty Images; (bottom) © Digital Vision/Getty Images.

Designer: Geri Fletcher